WAR
AND
PEACE
WITH
CHINA

DACOR PRESS

DACOR-BACON HOUSE

WAR AND PEACE WITH CHINA

First-Hand Experiences in the Foreign Service of the United States

MARSHALL GREEN
JOHN H. HOLDRIDGE
WILLIAM N. STOKES

Diplomatic and Consular Officers, Retired

DACOR-BACON
HOUSE

Published by DACOR Press
4858 Cordell Avenue
Bethesda, Maryland 20814-3011

Library of Congress Catalog Number 94-067959
Green, Marshall; Holdridge, John H.; and Stokes, William N.
War and Peace with China: First-Hand Experiences in the
Foreign Service of the United States
1st Edition

International Standard Book Number 1-885965-00-1

To our Foreign Service colleagues
who have labored in professional anonymity
to achieve peace and cooperation with China.

ACKNOWLEDGEMENTS

To Lisa, Martha, and Jadwiga for invaluable advice and support of this project and a lifetime of partnership in the experiences we recount.

To William Edmondson and Robert Miller, DACOR presidents present and future, for advice, encouragement and sponsorship of this effort to explain the role of the Foreign Service.

To William E. Knight, FSO retired, author and publisher, for skillfully editing our separate contributions into a cohesive whole.

To Morris Cobern, Allied Printing and Business Services, Bethesda, for ably shepherding a shower of drafts into this form.

To Professors Zhang Hsuguang and Chen Jian, Chinese Historians in the United States, for illuminating "the other side of the moon."

Cover design by Barbara Connolly.

Photographs are from authors' files.
Photo on page 182 by Martha Holdridge.

To order additional copies of this book photocopy and return the form below.

FOREWORD

In this book three US Foreign Service officers with key' roles in pivotal events affecting US–China relations during the past fifty years recount and interpret their firsthand experiences:

William Stokes took part in the early overtures to the Mao forces when they occupied Mukden in 1948 and in negotiations while he was under house arrest for a year. He served in Tokyo under MacArthur and Ridgway during the Korean War. From 1967 to 1973 he was deputy and then principal coordinator of US interagency advice to the Thai Government in its struggle against Maoist insurgency and Vietnamese raids on US bases. He is author of *Manufacturing Equity Joint Ventures in China*.

Marshall Green was from 1956 to 1965 successively Regional Planning Adviser for East Asia, Consul General in Hong Kong, and coordinator of efforts to modify US policy toward China. As Ambassador to Indonesia he witnessed collapse of the Indonesian Communist Party and the ouster of Sukarno—both major setbacks for Maoist policy. Later as Assistant Secretary of State for East Asia he accompanied President Nixon to China in 1972 which led to signing of the Shanghai Communique and its definition of the foundation for peace between the US and China.

John Holdridge, a Chinese-language officer, was a China-watcher at strategic posts for much of his early career. As senior staff member for East Asia in the National Security Council he worked directly for Henry Kissinger on the secretive negotiation of peace with China and then, as deputy to George Bush in Beijing, with its evolution into normal relations. Later, as Assistant Secretary of State for East Asia he helped to define the US–China relationship under President Reagan.

Warning: Memoirs focus on the role of the author, while history results from the actions of many. The perspective of an individual is necessarily partial. Yet eyewitness testimony puts flesh on the bones of history and reveals the human dynamics at work.

CONTENTS

Each author presents his own experiences and interpretation, after consultation with colleagues, and is solely responsible for his contribution. The publisher takes no position on the content and bears no responsibility for the views expressed.

PART I

WAR AND
THREAT OF WAR

by William N. Stokes

RUSSIA

HEILONGJIANG

MONGOLIA

Harbin

JILIN

INNER MONGOLIA

Xilin Hot

GANSU

Hohhot

HEBEI

LIAONING

NORTH

Dunhuang Jiayuguan

NINGXIA

Yellow River

Baotou

Datong

BEIJING

Shenyang

KOREA

Tianjin

Taiyuan

SHANXI

Yellow River

Jinan

SOUTH

QINGHAI

Lanzhou

SHANDONG

KOREA

YELLOW

Xi'an

Zhengzhou

SEA

SHAANXI

HENAN

JIANGSU

ANHUI

Nanjing

SICHUAN

HUBEI

Shanghai

Chengdu

Wuhan

Yangtze River

Hangzhou

Yangtze River

ZHEJIANG

EAST CHINA SEA

Changsha

JIANGXI

GUIZHOU

HUNAN

BURMA

Kunming

Guilin

FUJIAN

TAIWAN

YUNNAN

GUANGXI

GUANGDONG

Guangzhou (Canton)

VIETNAM

Hongkong

LAOS

SOUTH CHINA SEA

THAILAND

HAINAN

CHAPTER 1

THE US OFFERS AND
MAO REJECTS THE MIDDLE PATH

On Thanksgiving of 1946, when I landed in Shanghai, China was elated over the defeat of Japan and the prospective reunion of its land and people torn apart and humiliated for two centuries by seven colonial powers. Reality soon depressed the outlook. Civil war with the Communists dominated priorities of the government, as both fought to control strategic areas vacated by the Japanese. My assignment to Shenyang (formerly Mukden), center of Northeast China and capital of the old Manchu Empire, would bring me directly into the combat area.

US policy for this region was torn by conflicting objectives. In favor of continuing assistance to the government was the paramount aim of ending Russian military occupation, which showed signs of trying to maintain a permanent presence. So, in order to restore Chinese sovereignty over the Northeast the US assisted the advance of the national army by guarding the rail lines.

US misgivings were severe. During the war against Japan the US had received realistic reports of the Communist military potential and political skills from the Dixie Mission to Party headquarters in Yenan, in which Foreign Service officers like John Stewart Service participated along with military advisers. The advance of government forces into the Northeast was contrary to US military advice, which foresaw the resulting over-extension and inability to protect lines of supply.

President Truman demonstrated the importance the US attached to unifying China by means other than single-minded support of the governing party, the Kuomintang. He appointed General George C. Marshall, the architect of Allied victory, to mediate the civil war. Marshall formed a tri-partite Executive Headquarters, comprising US conciliators and both Chinese parties, with their ostensible cooperation.

This effort was hotly debated in US politics. One school held that the Chinese Communist Party (the CCP) was inevitably a tool of Stalin's policy of revolutionary expansion backed by military force. An opposing view held that the CCP might adopt a pragmatic middle path, giving priority to reconstruction. The Truman Administration was guided by Marshall toward the latter view, based on his positive first-hand experience in dealing with Zhou Enlai as CCP representative in the Executive Headquarters.

In a strategic sense the Truman administration was trying to dissuade the CCP from opting for an exclusive alliance with Moscow, by appealing to the Chinese penchant for practicality and reserve toward all foreign influences. The China Lobby in the US and the Republican Party, perceiving Communism to be essentially monolithic, considered the Administration effort foredoomed and possibly subversive.

The stakes were high. Northeast China, long influential in East Asian history, had the region's richest combination of natural resources, agriculture and industry. (In 1940 it was the world's sixth largest producer of steel). Throughout this century repeated foreign invasions have been opposed by consistent pressure from the United States to maintain an international "Open Door" there to commerce, investment, and information. That policy was being tested by Russia, as it had been by Japan.

When Soviet forces occupied Manchuria as the Japanese were surrendering, they seized the leading businesses, banks and railroads of the region, declaring them Soviet owned.

They occupied the naval base of Port Arthur under terms of their treaty in 1945 with Chiang Kai-shek. They gutted the core of heavy industry, ripping out industrial equipment wholesale and exporting it to Russia. Meanwhile, Moscow steadfastly refused to admit U.S. consular representatives, even the proposed transfer to Shenyang of the American Consul General in Vladivostok. These actions lent color to fears that Russia intended to make Northeast China a Russian protectorate, like Eastern Europe.

Pursuing its traditional "Open Door" policy, Washington brought heavy international pressure through the United Nations for prompt withdrawal of the Russians. In early 1946 they finally agreed, which then raised the question of whether they would do so in favor of their presumed Chinese partisans, the Communists, on terms which could leave Russian control intact, by indirection.

In fact the Russians admitted military and political delegations of the Kuomintang to principal cities under their control, facilitating the subsequent Kuomintang takeover of the former capital, Changchun, and the economic center of the Northeast, Shenyang. This was one of many instances of cross purpose between Moscow and Chinese Communists.

The Kuomintang armies, equipped and trained by the US to fight the Japanese, were successful in driving the Chinese Communist army (the PLA) northward in an initial series of sharp conventional battles. The whole southeast of Manchuria was cleared, while defeated Communist forces fled across the Yalu into the safe haven of North Korea. There they were refitted and enabled to rejoin CCP forces in the North by lateral movement through Korea. This was a debt of the CCP to Kim Il-sung, to be repaid later.

The US pressed its conciliation effort in the Northeast. Despite skill and a year of perseverance, Marshall failed, primarily because the Kuomintang government pursued campaigns to seize the whole Northeast by force, contrary to its earlier commitment to the US peace-making initiative.

The US might have suspended military assistance, but domestic political forces made that a practical impossibility. There was intense conservative partisanship in the US Congress for even **expanding** military support of the Nationalist cause in the name of "Anti-Communism." When career China specialists demurred because they questioned the viability of the Kuomintang, based on hard pragmatic evidence, they were vilified and some were summarily dismissed from the Foreign Service.

Though I was spared as too junior, I tasted the rancor. Before leaving Washington for China I had attended a press conference in mid-1946 at which the Bureau of Far Eastern Affairs was labelled "The Red Cell in the State Department" by the Scripps–Howard chain of papers. In editorial commentary that chain saw the Foreign Service as facilitating Russian domination of China by failure to stress the imputed subservice of the CCP to Moscow.

Even such a remote post as Shenyang was affected by American political divisions over China. The Consul General, an imposing Russian specialist named Angus Ward, had no previous service in China and cultivated close ties to the Republican opposition in the US through William Bullitt, the shadow Secretary of State for candidate Dewey.

Yet Foreign Service discipline prevailed. Ward ran the post "by the book," with the virtue that he did not suppress or distort staff reporting. That made a difference, because the White House was then still attentive to field realities as a foundation for policy. (The later fiascoes of Vietnam and Central America would not have been likely, given such attentiveness, but these are other stories.)

Our reporting clearly revealed substantial local trends disruptive of Communist international unity. From the arrival of Chinese Communist elements in the Northeast there had been severe tension with Soviet occupation forces. Residents showed me handbills distributed by the Soviet Commandant ordering all Chinese Communist forces out of Shenyang and gave me graphic accounts of numerous nocturnal assassinations of Soviet personnel.

Anti-Russian tension on the Communist side at levels below Mao, and great popular enthusiasm for restoration of Chinese sovereignty, created an opportunity for the incoming national government to form a broad coalition based on nationalism and widespread anti-Russian feeling.

The opportunity was squandered. The Kuomintang administration gave little attention to forming a political support structure in the Northeast, which had long been isolated from Intramural China (that is, inside the Great Wall). It discriminated systematically against native Northeasterners, preferring to rely at all levels on officials and troops from South China, which dominated the Kuomintang as a result of the long Japanese occupation of the North and the Northeast. Offers of support from local militias were rejected on smug grounds that they had been part of the colonial system.

The government brought about its own demise by these attitudes, which led to its increasing isolation. Within the leadership disgust at the harsh local climate and prolonged isolation from families led to brazen corruption manifest in large remittances to families in South China. The worst offenders were the military, who reported directly to the Generalissimo in Nanking and thus could circumvent and undermine the civil administration. It was a totally unworkable arrangement. Inflation became severe and cross-purposes were disabling.

The Communists, on the contrary, worked hard to merit local support by discipline and by recruiting militia and supporters of all political and ethnic origins. They especially appealed to those who had served Japan in local militias, whether "Manchukuo" or Korean origin. This historic and decisive move was reported, as it occurred, by Consul A. Sabin Chase, my mentor, in a message from Shenyang (Mukden) dated May 30, 1947. This and related messages, brilliantly synthesized and combined with other information by FSO Ralph Clough at the Embassy, demonstrated that the government had no future in the Northeast and documented the reasons therefor. These seminal reports, reproduced in the Department's White Paper *United States Relations with China*, gave the Department more than a year of warning about events to come.

From a longer perspective they justified the concerns about the viability of the Kuomintang regime that had been made during World War II by FSOs John Service, John Davies and other "Old China Hands." Their foresight and perseverance against "political correctness" cost them their careers but prepared official Washington for the coming sea change in China.

Korean volunteers and officers, mainly from two Chinese provinces northwest of the Yalu, joined the CCP in large numbers. They formed the 164th and 166th Divisions of the Fourth Army, were captors of Shenyang, and were among the most effective units of the Peoples Liberation Army. (Later they were to play a decisive secret role in Korea.)

As US advice had predicted, logistics and mobility considerations kept government forces restricted to cities and vulnerable lines of communication. Communist forces, changing strategy from direct confrontation, successfully applied hit-and-run tactics for which the terrain and climate were well suited. (These tactics, later enshrined in Mao's Handbook, were typical of measures which had won the

American Revolution, in the tradition of Marion, Rogers and Knowlton.)

The Government's crack divisions, primarily southerners, were intimidated by the region's Arctic winters and became increasingly passive. Soon even Shenyang, cut off from its fertile hinterland and rail supply from the South, began to starve.

A Secret Peace Initiative

At this juncture George Marshall, now Secretary of State, drew up a far-sighted plan to seek a *modus vivendi* with the Chinese Communists when events would bring them in contact with an American office. The plan remained secret, because opposition to any dealing with "Communists" continued to rage at home. But it was well founded in the Secretary's personal experience with Zhou Enlai, Mao's deputy, and with the perennial goal of US foreign policy: a China independent of foreign (then Russian) domination.

In late October 1948 the Nationalist regime abandoned Shenyang, the first major city to fall. Volunteers on the Consulate staff remained behind, according to the Marshall plan. When Mr. Ward's deputy, a Chinese language officer, left unexpectedly on the last plane, I succeeded him and was the only Chinese-speaking American left.

On November 3 the "Northeast Administrative Committee" of the CCP announced in the press a new municipal government. Mr. Ward immediately requested an audience with the Mayor, Zhu Qiwen, who was clearly the valid interlocutor we had been instructed to seek: he had come to Shenyang from being personal assistant to the overall Communist military and political leaders in the Northeast, who also were a members of the central Party Politburo.

In view of intense anti-American propaganda in the press, our hopes were not high. But the Mayor received us on November 5; moreover, we were invited in ostentatiously ahead of the local Soviet representation that had been waiting in the anteroom. I remember being totally surprised, and the faces of the Soviets reflected **their** shock.

The Consul General faithfully executed the peace initiative. He began by offering to respect local laws and regulations, and requested approval for normal functioning of our Consulate, including protection of American commercial activity. The Mayor vigorously assented: "We agree to your continuing consular function: we need Japanese industrial parts for our factories, which have been stripped by the Russians. You control Japan which needs to sell, so we can cooperate if we treat each other as equals." At our specific request, he promised diplomatic pouch privileges and protection for American business.

Again beyond our expectations, the Mayor on November 9 made a cordial return visit to the Consulate General, at which he reinforced the main themes for cooperation. Similar views were expressed to us by the new local manager of the Bank of China when we made a routine bank visit to obtain local currency. There seemed little doubt that the new Chinese position had been approved at a very high level.

We were overjoyed at these responses for their immediate promise of a "Reopen Door." The unequivocal positiveness and specific assurances of the Mayor's response were the more unexpected because they ran counter to the popular American assumption of a monolithic Sino-Soviet alliance and a tightly united top leadership of the CCP.

But then came a bombshell. On November 14, the British, French and American representatives each received a communication from the garrison commander, as head of the "Military Control Committee," addressing each as "The

Former Consul General." The circular letter demanded surrender of all radio transmitters (which only we Americans possessed).

In hope that this was an error, subordinate to the Mayor's repeated explicit recognitions of the Consulate General as such, we sought to involve the Mayor, but there was no response. We called upon the Garrison Commander with a conciliatory request for time to consult the US Government, offering meanwhile to cease transmissions. This could have been sufficient to allay any fears, if there had been a desire for continued dialogue.[1]

However, we were crudely rebuffed, with insistence on surrender of all equipment immediately. The next day troops surrounded the American Consulate General, seized its radio equipment, and held the staff *incommunicado* for a year under strict house arrest. Demonstrators with hostile placards (but curiously friendly gestures from their bearers) were paraded by.

Thus within five days we witnessed a major change of Communist policy in foreign relations, from recognition and welcome of consular functions to explicit non-recognition and peremptory control by force. We now know from Party documents that Mao had sought and obtained Russian advice on how to handle the Shenyang consulate, even before the city was taken, and carried it out exactly through the Garrison Commander.

During the secret visit of Soviet Politburo member Anastas Mikoyan to China in early 1949, Mao made clear that the Party's harsh tactics toward Western diplomats was responsive to its alliance with the Soviet Union. "Strategic relations between Communist China and the Soviet Union could be said to have begun with the Ward incident," states Professor Chen Jian from his close study of Party documents. Clearly Mao's fateful choice of strategic options was taken first, and the Ward affair was its earliest public manifestation.[2]

The Mayor, initially acting to the contrary, was following local guidance from the highest Northeast authorities, who evidently had a considerable reserve about cooperation with Russia and/or saw much to be gained by an opening to foreign trade. Mao personally criticized the Mayor for his discussions with us and ordered the silencing of consular communications. In doing so Mao was carrying out his strategic plan of cooperation with Russia to advance the Communist system, in China and (we would soon learn) beyond.[3]

A Fateful Choice

As the Communist Party began to taste victory in the long civil war, it faced a crucial choice between strategies for the paramount task of "Building the Nation." In the Party's own terminology the options were:

1) **"The Capitalist Road"** — Reconstruction of industry and commerce in their historical sites, the coastal cities and valleys, building on the colonial heritage. For this course international cooperation with maritime powers would be essential. Priority would be given to consolidating control of all China.

Supporters of this path were members of the Democratic League, overseas Chinese (a delegation from Hong Kong visited Shenyang and endorsed this course), and some tendencies within the Party (judging from the eloquence to us of Zhu Qiwen and his associates, in voicing such a clear rationale for trade with the US and Japan). Zhu's position, we now know, was approved in advance by Chen Yun, then deputy chief of the Northeast Commission and later to become a top national figure in the Party.

Allied by tactics to this opinion were the important Communist leaders who were disillusioned with the Russians (for their designs on Chinese territory and industrial larcenies in the Northeast). Several members of the Central Committee were later identified by the Party, after Mao turned against them, as "anti-Soviet ringleaders in the Northeast Plenum."[4]

2) **"Completing the Revolution"** —Priority for collectivizing agriculture and new heavy industry on a Socialist model, in the undeveloped interior where there would be security from foreign invasion and bombing. Military momentum to destroy Kuomintang remnants on Taiwan and their allies in Korea to be sustained by close association with Russia, which would supply the military and economic wherewithal.

Mao, endowed earlier with the power of unilateral decision in strategic matters, opted decisively for the second course. Even before the capture of Shenyang he had sought and obtained Soviet assistance in managing the economy of large cities. He underlined his strategic choice to the Party leadership and later to the public in an historic speech broadcast June 30, 1949, seven months after reversing cooperation with Western Consulates in the Northeast: "We must lean either to the Left or to the Right; there is no middle course."

In the speech he forecast the advent of world communism and, in a departure from his earlier Party positions cool to disciples of Moscow (like Li Lisan), acknowledged Russian inspiration for the Chinese Party. The Chairman went on to rebut at length each of the arguments for cooperation with the West earlier expressed to us in Shenyang by Mayor Zhu. Mao concluded bluntly: "In an era when imperialism still exists, it is impossible for a genuine people's revolution in any country to achieve victory without various forms of help from the international revolutionary forces. Even when victory is won, it cannot be made secure without such help.''[5] Soviet aid experts began arriving a month later.

Why did Mao take this unpopular tack, in the face of widespread anti-Russian sentiment in general and bitter resentment at Russian stripping of Manchurian industry in particular? The Chairman evidently was playing for high stakes: succession to Stalin as leader of international Communism, at least in Asia, and fulfillment of his folk slogan, ''The East is Red.''

In this light we can comprehend the full significance of the developments in Shenyang. From the US government viewpoint, an overture for peaceful cooperation sponsored at the highest level was rejected by China, in a brutal manner showing no interest in dialogue or conciliatory gestures from the US side — which had been made at high risk in domestic politics, where the opposition was condemning any dealings with Communism.

American About-Face

By mid-May 1949 the US realized that the original promise of dialogue had evaporated, and so ordered home the Shenyang staff of twelve Americans and Mrs. Ward, the lone dependent. (Before the city fell I had sent my wife, Jadwiga, home on the last plane to leave.)

The Chinese allowed this instruction to reach its destination, the first break in the *incommunicado* phase of detention. However, when the Consul General asked for transportation to leave Shenyang there was no answer. The Chinese side thereby avoided an opportunity for quiet resolution of the impasse and further embarrassed those American leaders who had sought a real dialogue with China.

The State Department then for the first time publicly protested our continued detention. Still no movement. Evidently Beijing now was seeking a self-justifying context for its actions, the more important because they had been imposed at the highest level. On June 19, the Chinese press reported discovery of a "spy ring" in Shenyang, with alleged ties to the Consulate General.

This charge was followed in ten days by disclosure of Mao's "Lean to the Left" justification of policy. The Chinese press made no mention of the house arrest of the American staff and the government made no move until the US brought international pressure.

On October 1 the new People's Government of China was promulgated. All of the 30-odd missions in Beijing, including the American, received a letter from Zhou Enlai requesting recognition. On October 10 the US replied with a note reviewing the detention of the Shenyang staff, again demanding its release.

Then matters moved so swiftly as to suggest an orchestrated provocation. The next day, on October 11, a Chinese employee of the Consulate General in Shenyang, who had been fired a month before for sleeping on the job, went to the Consul General's office against orders and demanded retirement compensation. Mr. Ward led him by the ear out to the main door. As an eyewitness, I can attest that no harm was done to the employee, although he was visibly frightened, and physical contact in such confrontations was abnormal by Chinese cultural standards.

On the stairs the Consul General was met in silent protest by the Chinese staff (choreography could explain their sudden and unprecedented assembly, given the nightly indoctrination sessions they had been subjected to for months). Then police arrived, taking the Consul General and three assistants away to jail.

In Mr. Ward's absence leadership fell to me. We were able to reopen communications with the State Department by inducing our captors to transmit an open message to Washington saying "all is well," knowing that my signature and the serial number (showing great gaps since the last message received in Washington a year earlier) would convey tacitly the essence of the situation.

The prisoners were returned to house arrest on November 13, after a three-hour trial which I was allowed to attend as an observer. There was no examination of the Americans or opportunity for defense. After a ten minute recess the chief judge read a ten page printed set of findings. The severe sentence of forced labor was superseded, "in view of the seriousness of the offense," by an order for immediate deportation.

Two days after the expulsion order I was invited to and did attend, again as an observer, another showcase trial which dealt with allegations of spying. It deserves examination because some American critics still hypothesize that US espionage was a **cause** of the Chinese policy reversal toward the Consulate. That view doesn't take account of the actual sequence of events.

In August 1948, before Shenyang was occupied, the personal representative of Stalin to Mao, Kovalev,[6] alleged to Mao that the American Consulate in Shenyang was gathering tactical military information about the Communist forces and relaying it to the Nationalist command. He recommended that the Communist side, once Shenyang was captured, blockade the Consulate, seize its radio station, and not allow its staff to leave. Russian advice was followed to the letter.

The allegation of military complicity is not credible. The single US military attache at the Consulate, Captain David

Longacre, had no field staff. The information he reported to Washington was what he picked up from the Kuomintang forces. In disgust at the uselessness of his mission, he had been called home six months previously. In any case, the US had for years abandoned any interest in guiding Nationalist forces (who had ignored US advice in entering the Northeast in the first place).

Nor was the evidence later produced in court any more convincing of real threat to Chinese security. The accused were a Japanese, a Mongol, and a Chinese worker, none of whom could have had access to Chinese military or state secrets. Americans were not named as defendants, even *in absentia.*

That is not to deny some routine efforts to obtain information clandestinely. The materiel displayed apparently was American. The trial cited "External Survey Detachment #44, US Army" as organizer from the US side. I happened to live in the Standard Oil Company compound where this organization had its offices until it left, well before the Kuomintang administration collapsed. None of the staff had Chinese language capability.

That was because the main target of US intelligence was the local Russian representation. Activities of Soviet agents in Northeast China had concerned the US and led to development of information sources about them. To my knowledge, such intelligence collection was merely part of the "background clutter" of events in the wake of a recent war and Soviet occupation, not of a nature to affect high international policy. In effectiveness was serio-comic as regards the Chinese, who could have had no serious worries about their own security.

To their credit, the Chinese never officially claimed otherwise. The charges and trial did serve to appease the Russians, as shown by Party documents, and to "justify" Mao's option for alliance with Russia. Surely that was their explanation.

With neither trial did all Chinese officials necessarily feel they had an adequate explanation under international practice for detention of the Shenyang staff. Philip Manhard, a member of the Consulate General in Tianjin that arranged details of our deportation, recalls receiving an apology from senior officials disavowing the treatment of the Shenyang consular staff as "not in accord with central government policy." Whether this was a sign of internal dissent or a propaganda ploy is hard to tell: one might discount it except for accurate disclosures to Manhard soon thereafter, about the imminence of war in Korea.

Our trip south to Tianjin by train, under armed guard, on the night of December 6 was sidetracked frequently by heavy traffic going north, quite likely Chairman Mao's own special train to Moscow that very night.

A few weeks later, the British and French Consuls in Shenyang were, without explanation, also ordered out of the Northeast (the British even though they were recognizing the People's Republic). Access was denied to all visitors. The Northeast was being made ready for its new strategic role, about to be revealed.

The Pauley Mission inspects the Anshan Steel Works, stripped of key equipment by Russian Forces, although (or because) it was critical to reconstruction of Northeast China (October 1946).

Consul General Angus Ward with Army Captain David Longacre, the only military member of Consulate General Shenyang when Stalin accused it of guiding Kuomintang combat campaigns (September 1947).

Professional Chinese staff in the American Consulate General, Shenyang: Roger Hsu, Zhang Peiju, and Ma Yukwei formed an essential link between our two nations before Mao's decision to place Americans under guard and sequester locals (May 1948). Zhang served in Gen. Marshall's Executive Headquarters and later in Consulate General Hong Kong.

Jadwiga Stokes about to leave Shenyang on the last flight, hours before the city's capture, October 26, 1948.

Typical demonstration in front of American Consulate Shenyang. Lenin and Engels on banners decrying "US imperialism" (above). US Consulate (lower right) under armed guard while a demonstration passes (June 1949).

Truman Brands Ward Arrest By Reds In Mukden As 'Outrage'

WASHINGTON, Nov. 17—(Reuter)—President Truman today branded as an outrage the Chinese Communist arrest of the American consul general, Angus Ward, at Mukden, Manchuria. He made his denunciation of the Red action at a news conference soon after announcing plans for an extraordinary conference of all top U.S. diplomats in the Far East.

The meeting, to be held at Bangkok, Siam, in late January, will devise strategy for holding the Asiatic line against Communist expansion. It is the first such parley in the Pacific area as the Red armies begin overrunning China and menacing all Asia.

Chances Spoiled

Mr. Truman did not elaborate on his statement, but he pointedly called attention to the statement of the Secretary of State, Dean Acheson, yesterday that the incident had killed any chance of the United States granting diplomatic recognition to the Communist regime in China. Mr. Ward and four of his consulate employees have been held incommunicado somewhere in Mukden since October 24 and efforts of U.S. officials to contact him have been fruitless.

Reporters advised President Truman that the British former Prime Minister, Mr. Winston Churchill, had urged that both Britain and the U.S.A. extend "de facto" recognition to the Communists. The President replied that Mr Churchill was entitled to his own opinion, and that he would not comment on the suggestion.

U.S. Consulates

The State Department, meanwhile, moved to close the United States' diplomatic offices in Chungking and Kunming, China, in the face of new Communist advances. The conference announcement was made by the White House after Mr. Truman had reviewed the steadily worsening Far Eastern situation at an 80-minute closed meeting with the Secretary of State, Dean Acheson, the U.S. Ambasador at large, Philip Jessup, and other high officials. Dr. Jessup, who heads the new State Department Far Eastern policy group, will attend the Bangkok session and bring back a full report to Mr. Truman and Mr. Acheson. He will also visit Japan, India and Pakistan and possibly other Asiatic trouble spots.

Hongkong Standard, November 19, 1949

SOUTH CHINA MORNING POST, SUNDAY NOVEMBER 20, 1949

DETENTION OF CONSUL

Mounting U.S. Indignation Over Angus Ward's Case

STRONG PRESS CRITICISM

Washington, Nov. 18.

The State Department reported to-day that all its efforts to make effective contact with the Chinese Communist authorities on the Angus Ward case had thus far failed.

Speculation persisted here that one of the next moves might be an appeal to the Russians for aid in obtaining the release of the gaoled Consul-General at Mukden. But the State Department maintained strict silence on its plans.

The latest report from the Vice-Consul, Mr William N. Stokes, at Mukden showed that, Mr Ward and the four staff members arrested with him on October 24 were still imprisoned, and possibly themselves had no hope of early release. They had asked for reading materials.

Mr Stokes' message, dated November 16 and relayed through the American consulate at Mukden, said Mr Ward had asked for five books and five magazines for the imprisoned group and also for fresh supplies of food and clothing. These evidently are to replace those which had been used up by the detained men during the past three and one half weeks. The message said they had sent out soiled clothes to be laundered.

Mr Fulton's Offer

The State Department's official disclosure of the complete failure of its efforts to date came in the course of a reply made to Representative James C. Fulton, Republican, on an offer he had made to serve as hostage for Mr Ward. Mr Fulton said he acted in hope it would bring about a definite policy for protection of American officials.

The reply was telephoned to Mr Fulton by the Special Assistant Secretary of State, Mr Lucius D. Battle. The substance of what Mr Battle told Mr Fulton was then made public by the Press officer, Mr Michael McDermott.

In the conversation, Mr McDermott said, Mr Battle informed Mr Fulton that to exchange him for Mr Ward would "merely constitute an exchange of individuals in an unchanged, extremely serious situation.

"The Department has no reason to believe," Mr McDermott's version of the conversation continued, "that the Chinese Communists would be willing to accept the Congressman as a hostage for Mr Ward against whom the Communists have brought specific charges and in view of our inability to make effective contact with the Communist authorities, it is not known how practicable contact could be made for this purpose."

At the same time Mr Battle reiterated the State Department's frequently declared assurances that it is "currently doing everything possible to secure the release of Mr Ward and the other staff members being held in gaol and to arrange for the prompt repatriations of all the American personnel of the Consulate General".

Letter to Brother

Last July, Mr Ward wrote to his brother Mr T. R. Ward of Allegan, that he "expected almost anything." The brother now is in Washington conferring with State Department officials about the case.

"It is my opinion," the Consul wrote, "that the local authorities in their zeal of apply-ing the boot and club to us, are doing their government great disservice for the reason that a day of reckoning will certainly come. They will be made to realise that barbarities cannot be practised to-day in in e n tional usage without creating repercussions."

"As for myself," the Consul added, "I can take whatever is ladled out to me and even derive a reasonable modicum of fun from it."

A year ago, the Consul asked his brother to find an apartment in America for himself and his wife when they were able to leave China.—Associated Press.

New York's morning papers, according to *United Press*, discussing the Ward case and the question of recognition of the Chinese Communist Government, asked further Government efforts for the release of Mr Angus Ward.

The *Times*, referring to Mr Ernest Bevin's House of Commons statement said: "Mr Bevin cannot suppose there will be substantial support in this country for United States recognition of the Communist regime so long as that regime pursues policies of piracy, brigandage and blackmail in respect of United States citizens and United States officials.

"It is safe to suggest that the discussion of recognition would not be calm and collected in the House of Commons if it were the British Consul who is in the Mukden gaol and British citizens who are held as hostages in North Korea."

The paper again referred to the formal Chinese Nationalist government charges against the Soviet Union of treaty violations and abetment of aggression.

The editorial said: "Neither the United States nor the United Kingdom can ignore those charges, however embarrassing they may be to the International Assembly. Action at this time in derogation of the Chinese Government and in recognition of the Chinese Communists would rightly be regarded as prejudgment on the case in favour of the Soviet Union."

The first meal in freedom, ending 13 months of detention. Aboard the Lakeland Victory in Taku, L/R: Fred Hubbard, Mary Braden, Hugo Picard, William Stokes, Ralph Rehberg.

The Shenyang party of freed detainees flanking Consul General and Mrs. Ward, including (in addition to those cited above), Elden Erickson, Jack Feigel, Shiro Tatsumi and family, Alfred Kristan and Franco Cicogna. (December 8, 1949).

CHAPTER 2

WAR IN KOREA:
THE EMPERORS LOCK HORNS

We now know, from heretofore secret records, that in Moscow Mao applied his policy of Communist solidarity through a series of agreements, including a treaty of mutual defense.

During Mao's visit the Soviet leadership was secretly preparing to extend Communist control throughout Korea by military means. (Kim Il Sung made the long trip to Moscow four times in 1949-50, and was there for the most active stage of Stalin-Mao discussions in February 1950.) While Stalin had few if any compunctions about deceiving an ally, he could not afford an alienated China, especially during an Asian conflict. More positively, China's active cooperation would safeguard against the unexpected, such as a strong US reaction. It was typical of Stalin to let others take the main risk.

As we have shown, Mao had prepared his Party for cooperation with Russia before leaving for Moscow. Beijing would benefit by the removal of South Korea as an ally of Taiwan, but the main thrust was strategic cooperation with the USSR in achieving the spread of Communism in Asia by force and subversion.

Khrushchev's memoirs and those of Mao's entourage confirm the fact of Stalin-Mao discussions about Korea during Kim's presence in Moscow. The consensus was that the Americans would not intervene against the planned invasion. Even if Mao only accepted the assurance of others, he made the same misjudgment of the US that MacArthur was soon to make about China.

While Mao was still in Moscow there was another major US effort to dissuade him from all-out commitment to Stalin. President Truman in January 1950 renounced the use of force in the civil war in China, notably in Taiwan. There was no response from Beijing, and Mao plunged ahead regardless.

China's Military Involvement from the Start

The general understanding of the public is that China entered the Korean war in response to the US invasion of the North, but that belief is contradicted by recent disclosures in China, through memoirs of leading Chinese participants, referring to messages from Mao to his field commanders.

From these solid sources we now know:

In late 1949, even before Mao's visit to Moscow, two divisions of the Chinese New Fourth Army, mainly composed of ethnic Koreans, were sent to Korea with their equipment, in organized units under orders, and took up forward positions.[3]

In January 1950, while Mao was in Moscow, all remaining ethnic Koreans in the Chinese Liberation Army, another 40,000 or so, were sent to Korea and organized into the Seventh Division of the "Korean Peoples' Army," which spearheaded the original attack. (From the memoirs of the Chinese commander in Korea, General Nie Rongzhen, Beijing 1984).

The overpowering character of the North Korean attack on the South, six months later, becomes more understandable because the units committed by Mao were among the most effective in the Chinese Army. They constituted perhaps half of the attacking force. Also, many of the Korean general officers in the invasion had long experience in the Chinese civil war.

The attack was spearheaded by 150 of the famous Russian T-34 main battle tanks that had beaten the Panzers at Stalingrad. The invasion battle plan was drawn up by North Korea with direct Soviet military participation. Thus the invasion of South Korea was hardly a civil war: it was manned, supplied and organized by a triple alliance of Communist states.

Advance Warning

Another common belief is that the US had no advance knowledge of the Communist attack in Korea. In fact, the Foreign Service in China reported specific evidence of Mao's intentions in Korea.[7] In April 1950, six weeks after Mao's return from Moscow and two months before the invasion, Manhard in Tianjin was given stunning information by the Director of the Export/Import Organization, a highly placed Party official and therefore much more powerful than his nominal post in government would indicate. He said a war would soon break out in Korea, backed by the USSR and the Peoples' Republic of China: "Chinese forces are already moving north through Tianjin."(These were apparently the mainly ethnic Korean units of the Chinese Army mentioned above.)

But the CIA, to which the Department had referred this report, did not credit what proved to be a superb example of crucial intelligence, perhaps because it had been openly arrived at. Nor did the Department take action.

The report was confirmed specifically after the event. During later interrogations in Korea by Manhard, POWs from China reported that their units had been moved suddenly to the Manchurian borders of Korea at this time from their training grounds in Intramural China, where they had been preparing for an invasion of Taiwan.

Thus by supplying major, battle-hardened forces and their equipment, Mao made China an important if concealed participant in the original invasion of Korea, from planning to execution. We have traced a linear and consecutive relationship in 1949 between Mao's brutal rejection of Secretary Marshall's peace overture, arrest of its messengers in Shenyang, and China's early commitment to armed aggression in Korea. All three were linked elements of Mao's grand strategy for domination of East Asia through a concerted international Communist military campaign, initially under the guise of "national liberation" by North Korean surrogates.

Stalin was the prime mover in planning the original Korean invasion, but Mao was a willing and major participant, in a curiously derivative manner, with fateful consequences for US–China relations.

The US in Japan

Was the American theater commander concerned about the danger of a Chinese-supported attack? During a transit stop in Japan by the Shenyang staff on their way home, General MacArthur gave us a private luncheon. To our surprise the General lectured us about "chaos" in China as requiring greater US assistance for Chiang Kai-shek. When the Consul General disagreed, by pointing out the great extent to which American aid had fallen into Communist hands, the General departed abruptly without inquiring about our recent experience. History would turn on such deafness to Chinese realities.

The American press, also oblivious to the impending storm, gave heavy play to the human interest aspects of our confinement, which President Carter was later to term America's first postwar experience with hostage-taking. My compensation was reunion in New York on January 4, 1950 with my wife Jadwiga and my son Brian, born during my detention.

All too soon thereafter, the Deputy Director for Northeast Asian Affairs, U. Alexis Johnson, recruited me to do peripheral reporting in Tokyo on developments in China. This assignment brought me in contact with wartime leaders of industry and diplomacy, who retained great interest in their former colonies. Admiral Nomura Kichisaburo, envoy to Washington at the time of Pearl Harbor, described the progressive enmeshment of Japanese ground forces in the invasion of intramural China in 1937. "At first the Army asked the War Council for authority to commit 250,000 troops, insisting that would suffice. By several increments the request reached five million, and victory was always just beyond reach." What an augury for our campaigns in Vietnam!

Before the Korean surprise attack, American attention in Asia was focussed on the tasks of peace. The occupation of Japan introduced reforms so radical as to invite doubt about their potential to survive a peace treaty. In fact, they have been absorbed by the Japanese into their own miracle of becoming a world power, including such liberal concepts as civil rights for women, land reform, parliamentary democracy, and renunciation of force.

There was a parallel miracle on the American side: liberal reforms promulgated by a great American conservative,

General MacArthur, and the confirming Peace Treaty negotiated by another, John Foster Dulles —both operating under a Democratic White House. Such bipartisanship preserved American relations with Japan from the internal political squabbles which so rent and beclouded our relations with China.

Korea Explodes

Like a bolt from the blue combined Communist forces in June 1950 attacked South Korea, whose underarmed and surprised forces crumbled. Unprepared US elements from Japan had to be thrown in piecemeal.

In committing US forces President Truman also ordered the US Navy to interdict the Taiwan strait, to protect from a potential Chinese invasion. Was this a provocation of Mao, **causing** China to become involved directly in Korea, as some observers have inferred?

Because Mao had already involved China deeply, the American action was much more a reaction than a provocation. Moreover, involvement of the US Navy in a measure to contain potential hostilities around Taiwan arose from the Pentagon's explicit concern that World War III might be impending — a fear which was more realistic than was understood at the time, in view of the international character of the attack. (The USSR had exploded its first nuclear device months later.)

At this fevered point, Secretary Acheson made a crucial move toward restraint by refusing to accept Chiang Kai-shek's offer of 33,000 Nationalist troops to fight with the US in Korea. This was the third American initiative reduce or limit differences with China which Mao ignored, after the

Marshall initiative in Shenyang and the Truman offer on Taiwan in January.

On July 7, a fortnight after the initial attack, when it was still in full promise of total victory, Mao constituted the Northeast Border Defense Army to prepare "an intervention in the Korean War if necessary." On August 4, while American forces were still retreating toward Pusan, Mao told a Politburo meeting that China needed to help North Korea with military volunteers.

The next day Mao ordered his border army to complete preparations for war operations in Korea by September. His internal communications show that his consistent purpose was the complete eviction of US forces from Korea. He issued this order **before** the Inchon landing and defeat of the North Korean forces: it is explicit in Mao's messages that he was not responding to any American threat or peace offer, but was aiming at total triumph by military means.

Events would soon justify Acheson's caution about military cooperation with Taiwan, by proving it redundant. After the invaders had pushed the allies to the southern point of Korea, MacArthur's successful landing at Inchon in late August led to complete reversal of the tri–partite aggression when the original boundary at the 38th parallel was regained.

On September 14, Stalin cabled Mao asking for further Chinese military intervention. Mao gave orders to the Chinese Border Army to deploy into Korea on October 2, five days before US forces crossed the 38th parallel. In doing so he overrode majority opposition in the Politburo. He even persevered a week later when Zhou Enlai was informed in Moscow by Stalin that the earlier Soviet offer of air cover was withdrawn, a lack that was to cost China the war.[8]

At this point MacArthur committed the same sin of overconfidence and ignorance of the opposing side that Mao had just displayed. Not satisfied with victory but intent on triumph, MacArthur began a rapid advance to the Chinese border although he had assured President Truman at Wake Island that the Chinese would not intervene. Foreign Service voices spoke out in alarm. "Bohlen, Kennan, and a few Old China Hands warned that Beijing or Moscow would not tolerate US violation of the 38th parallel."[9]

The White House urgently sought independent field views. Ambassador John Muccio in Korea was isolated from the front and in no position to evaluate the MacArthur interpretation. A noted military historian, Trevor Dupuy, states that the CIA supported MacArthur's position, even though "The presence of Chinese troops in North Korea was undeniable (judging from battlefront intelligence and captives) at the very moment of MacArthur's assurance."[10]

On what, then, was MacArthur's assurance based? His open partisanship for Chiang Kai-shek on Taiwan evidently misled him into a profound underestimation of the new regime's capabilities as well as its intentions. After the Chinese presence in Korea became manifest, MacArthur estimated their strength at one tenth the actual number and pursued his advance. His wish was father to his thought.

To Mao's great delight, as revealed in telegrams to his commanders, MacArthur was falling into a terrible trap. Apparently he paid no more attention to his own battlefront intelligence than he had paid to the Shenyang staff a year before.

Why wasn't he countermanded? President Truman was never hesitant to make hard decisions. Certainly for US forces to occupy new territory on the mainland directly upon the Chinese frontier was not a mere tactical question within the purview of a field commander, even a Proconsul like MacArthur.

Reality in a democracy did not give the president such leeway. It was politically difficult to oppose MacArthur in the face of general disbelief that the Chinese were willing or able to intervene against US forces. Except for those who had witnessed the denouement of the Chinese civil war, few took the new China seriously, even as a defender of its immediate boundary areas. The president ordered MacArthur not to proceed unless certain the Chinese would not intervene, but even he could not challenge the hero of Inchon until more sure of his ground.

What about the warning that had been given Washington by Zhou Enlai, in an October message to the US through the Indian Foreign Minister, that Chinese intervention would follow an advance into North Korea?[11] It was not credited because the intermediary was not trusted, and in any case, as shown above, the message came too late. We now know that Mao was already committed to intervention, even before US forces crossed the original border between North and South on October 7. Mao so replied to Stalin's request in a telegram dated October 2: "We have decided to send a part of the armed forces into Korea. . . ."

The Chinese mass intervention was hugely successful because MacArthur: 1) misconstrued Chinese intentions, 2) over-rated the ability of US airpower to isolate the battlefield, and 3) underestimated Chinese military effectiveness. As a consequence, American casualties were severe. Only heroic discipline and valor during the retreat prevented destruction of the American forces as Mao had planned.

In the midst of a rout in which the Chinese captured Seoul, General Matthew Ridgway succeeded to field command and stabilized the front. Truman and Acheson then planned to offer China a negotiated settlement of differences (much as Marshall had done in Shenyang two years before).

Just as this offer was about to be conveyed, MacArthur on March 24 from his Tokyo headquarters destroyed its potential by an insulting and totally unauthorized demand for Chinese capitulation, threatening bombardment of the mainland. Given his close association with the Kuomintang on Taiwan, it was a threat to reopen the civil war. [12,13]

At this incredible insubordination, Truman removed MacArthur and replaced him in Tokyo with Ridgway. But the opportunity to offer peace (a fourth time!) had been ruined. There was no silencing MacArthur who on his triumphal return to the US again called for a naval blockade and air attacks on Chinese industrial centers. Would this hideous war become worse still?

In an unprecedented by-passing of what had been sacrosanct channels of command, General Ridgway summoned me to his private office in GHQ. He referred to my earlier reporting from Shenyang on railway operations and asked for comment about the proposed bombing of communications in Northeast China.

My response: the same Chinese armies engaged in Korea had defeated US-trained and equipped forces in Manchuria only two years before. They did so by successfully operating irregular lines of communication and supply while under unopposed air attack by American aircraft flown by American-trained pilots. Probably they could revert effectively to their old ways. Moreover, carrying the war to China proper would unite all Chinese in a national fervor, justifying Mao's decision to invade Korea.

Ridgway's investment of personal time and effort demonstrates his care to collect and face facts before arriving at conclusions, regardless of preconceptions. This quality of mind, so lacking in Mao and MacArthur, was marked in the pragmatists on both sides (most notably the later reversal of Maoism by Zhou Enlai and his successor, Deng Xiaoping).

Ridgway then recommended against bombing, based upon a wide variety of information and advice. His conclusion that a cross-border air campaign would not be decisive was later validated in Vietnam, where enormous tactical air campaigns against the Ho Chi Minh trail were unable to halt guerrilla resupply. Also, we now know that the USSR had promised China air defense of Manchuria if the US attacked (a substitute for its earlier offer of air cover in Korea, which had a higher degree of credibility because the stakes would have been so much higher.)

Accordingly, the war was not widened. After an extended stalemate, a truce was negotiated by President Eisenhower. War weariness, horror at the casualties and the change of partisan power in Washington precluded full appreciation at the time of what has been gained by the Truman decision to resist aggression.

Long Term Effects of the Korean War

With the passage of time we can see more clearly the effects of the war, particularly in light of the recent evidence about international Communist participation in the invasion.

1) **Effects on those who started the war:**
   The Soviet Union, while suffering no direct loss, saw its Asian protege North Korea weakened and isolated. More importantly, defeat of the joint enterprise with Mao undermined entente with China. One of the largest factors in failure of the Chinese intervention proved to be precisely the lack of promised Russian air cover, to which huge losses were directly attributable.

Chinese resentment of the Russians, long standing anyway, neared the boiling point, but built up inside a pressure–cooker because Mao was unwilling to admit error about his cooperation with Stalin. However, the eventual Sino–Soviet break had become inevitable.

By intervening openly in Korea China proved ability and readiness to defend its frontiers, largely silencing foreign extremists who had been calling for an invasion of the mainland from Taiwan. But there had only been bravado behind that proposal, which did not require a war with the US to dispel.

Mao personally, as prime author of the decision to cooperate militarily with the Russians, was the big loser in the Korean War. His avowed goal to destroy American forces and reunite Korea "in the Red" totally miscarried, weakening fatally his reputation as the "Great Helmsman." The direct cost of the Korean war was compounded for China by the consequence of economic isolation. Had China instead followed in 1948 the policy outlined to us by the Mayor of Shenyang, it could have gained a quarter century in the race among Asian countries for prosperity in a market economy.

The Chinese and the American "emperors," Mao and MacArthur, who were so much alike in being misled by their own initial success and in misjudgment of their opponents, declined in parallel. The impact on their societies of their failures differed widely because of the fundamental difference between the two political systems. MacArthur was stripped of power, whereas Mao could and did destroy his critics and went on to compound his error in Korea by increasingly abortive efforts to prove himself. The disaster of "The Great Leap Forward" and the horror of the Cultural Revolution marked successive steps toward his eventual obloquy among those who understood, although his image remained as an icon of continuity for the regime.

2) The Intended Victims

The United States in Korea achieved the objectives for which it entered the war: regaining invaded territory and defeating the invasion force. Today we can see that it laid the foundation for United Nations action to roll back aggression and keep the peace.

The Republic of Korea was enabled to come of age, soon to become a paragon of market-oriented development and eventually an example of democratic political reform on China's borders.

Japan was preserved from having a victorious and aggressive enemy coalition on its southern approaches, as a lower jaw to the Russian threat from the north. The real and present danger would have been encouragement of leftist sentiment in Japan and general disillusionment with the US alliance.

The Japanese economic miracle received an important initial impetus when its industry was awarded lucrative contracts to resupply US forces in Korea. From this source it accumulated vital investment capital and knowhow in the American market. At the governmental level, US grant assistance was continued well beyond the otherwise reasonable time to convert it to loans, or stop it altogether.

The serious threat that North Korea is still deemed to be, including a potential nuclear capability, was greatly diminished.

The Korean war ended with confusing compromise and war-weariness, which we are only now able to see through. What we are learning about the Sino-Russian collaboration and its purpose to Communize all of Korea validate the American decision to resist the attack. Failure to do so would have encouraged Mao and Stalin in their imperial ambitions and threatened Japan. Later exaggeration of such strategic factors to justify the Vietnam war should not obscure their applicability to the invasion of Korea, made evident by our recent information from Beijing and Moscow.

As for relations with China, the war left a residue of hostility and the future cloudy. Would the thorny issues remaining, especially the future of Taiwan, be the subject of renewed conflict? Under the circumstances, how could we consider, much less establish, a dialogue with China?

References

1.   Stokes, William N., *Diary of Events*, Foreign Services Despatches from Mukden, Oct 1948 to Dec 1949, US National Archives.

_____, "The Future Between America and China," *American Foreign Service Journal*, Washington, DC, Jan. 1968.

_____, et.al., *Manufacturing Equity Joint Ventures in China*, A.T. Kearney,Inc., Chicago, 1987.

United States Relations with China, pp 315-317, Mukden message of May 30, 1947, US State Dept, Washington, DC, 1949.

Steven I. Levine, *Anvil of Victory, The Communist Revolution in Manchuria, 1945-48*, Columbia Univ. Press, New York, 1984.

2. Chen Jian, "The Ward Case and the Emergence of Sino-American Confrontation, 1948-1950," *The Australian Journal of Chinese Affairs*, No. 30, Sydney, July 1993. (Based on Chinese Communist Party documents).

3. _____ "Origins of China's Intervention in the Korean War,"*Chinese Historians*, Winter 1993.

4. J.P.R.S. *Translations on International Communist Developments*, No. 605, May 27, 1964, on dissidence in the leadership.

5. Mao Zedong, *Selected Works IV*, pg 370.

6. Goncharov, S.N., "Stalin's Dialogue with Mao Zedong," *Journal of Northeast Asian Studies*, Winter 1991-92, pp 45ff.

7. Manhard, Philip, "Memorandum of Conversation," June 25, 1950, US National Archives.

8. Christensen, Thomas J., "Threats, Assurances and the Last Chance for Peace. (The Lessons of Mao's Korean War Telegrams)," *International Security*, 17:1, pp 122-154, Summer 1992.

    Clubb, O. Edmund, *20th Century China*, Third Ed., pg 267ff., Columbia Univ. Press, New York, 1978.

9. Halberstam, David, 1993, *The Fifties* pp 84 & 101ff, Villard, New York, 1993.

10. Dupuy, Trevor N., *Encyclopedia Britannica*, page 471, "Korean War," 1965.

11. Reston, James *Deadline*, 1992, page 385, Random House, New York 1991.

    Salisbury, Harrison, *The New Emperors*, Little, Brown, Boston, 1992.

12. Acheson, Dean *Present at the Creation*, Norton, New York, 1969.

13. McCullough, David, *Truman*, pp 790 ff, Simon & Schuster, New York, 1992.

    Goncharev, Lewis and Xue, *Uncertain Partners: Stalin, Mao and the Korean War*, Stanford, Palo Alto, 1994.

PART II

AVERTING WIDER WAR

by Marshall Green

CHAPTER 3

MANAGING THE TAIWAN CRISIS

The grudging settlement in Korea brought tension over Taiwan to the forefront of US concern when I rejoined the Far East Bureau as Regional Planning Advisor in 1956.

The Bureau was dominated by Assistant Secretary of State Walter Robertson, the quintessential Virginia gentleman, a banker by profession, who had powerful connections in the Administration and Congress. Robertson's overriding interest in world affairs was to uphold the position of Generalissimo Chiang Kai-shek as President of all of China, even though Chiang and his defeated Nationalist forces had fled the mainland in 1949 to take refuge on Taiwan. Because of Robertson's fixation on China, and because I had to draft a number of his speeches, I was automatically drawn into China policy issues, especially those relating to the defense of the Republic of China from the People's Republic of China, a term we rarely used in those days.

Robertson was kindly and thoughtful towards all members of his staff. He was also a strong defender of the Foreign Service at a time when many officers were still reeling from the effects of McCarthyism. All 14 of the ambassadors in his area (East Asia and Australasia) were career officers, a record never before or since achieved by any bureau in the State Department.

I was also fortunate in having Ambassador J. Graham Parsons as my immediate superior. He was Deputy Assistant Secretary of State at that time, and was to replace Robertson in 1959. Jeff Parsons was one of the ablest officers in the Foreign Service, articulate and a master of diplomatic practices, so essential in our business. On the other hand, Walter

Robertson's single-minded dedication to upholding the position of Chiang Kai-shek as the President of all of China was one I could not altogether share, and writing acceptable speeches taxed my New England conscience to its limits.

We also expended vast amounts of diplomatic capital on upholding Taibei's position in the United Nations as the sole legal representative of all of China; and our highly visible military presence on Taiwan, especially in the capital, was bound to affront nationalistic feelings. It certainly affronted the sensibilities of foreign diplomats like the Japanese ambassador who was billeted in a US military area in the center of Taibei identified on large billboards as "Freedom Village."

I happened to be visiting there in May of 1957 as a member of a Presidential Mission headed by Frank Nash, Assistant Secretary of Defense, which was looking into problems related to our worldwide base presence. Just as we were being reassured by the US Charge d'Affaires that there was no problem with the public over our base presence in Taiwan, our Embassy was attacked by a mob that sacked the Embassy, beat up some of our personnel hiding in the basement, and scattered official US files all over the streets.

This mob action was touched off by the shooting of a Taiwanese peeping-tom by an American sergeant, who was then acquitted by an American military court in Taibei amidst the cheers of his compatriots and in the presence of the peeping-tom's weeping widow and her friends. Armed with evidence like this, the Frank Nash mission came up with convincing conclusions and recommendations that did much, world-wide, to lessen friction about the presence of US bases overseas.

We gave close attention to evidence of a growing split in Sino-Soviet relations. I twice visited the Rand Corporation at Santa Monica, California, where a team of experts was analyzing Beijing's reactions to the launching of Sputnik in 1957. It was increasingly clear to these experts (including my former State Department colleague Alice Hsieh) that Chinese efforts to share in, and benefit from, Soviet technological breakthroughs were being rebuffed by Moscow. Two Chinese delegations returned to Beijing empty-handed. This was briefly followed by Chinese propaganda broadcasts calling for a nuclear-free Far East, but it was clear that this line, probably purveyed to Beijing by Moscow, was in conflict with Beijing's own aspirations to become a nuclear power.

It was not until the following year that I became directly involved in the formulation of US policy toward China, during and after the Taiwan Strait Crisis of 1958. At that time I became Secretary Dulles' action officer at the working level for these events. I shall describe this crisis in some detail because accounts I have read are incomplete with regard to how Washington policy makers grappled with it.

For several months before the Communists opened up their artillery barrage against Quemoy on August 23, 1958, I had been chairing a working-level interagency task force (State, Defense and CIA) which was one of several established by the White House to examine US capabilities to cope with two or more simultaneous military crises in various parts of the world. One of the scenarios our task force had just completed related to aerial or artillery interdiction of the Quemoy island group (Big Quemoy, Little Quemoy, Tatan, Ehrtan and Tungting) held by the Nationalists but located just a few miles off the shore of mainland China.

When in fact an artillery interdiction was launched against the Quemoy group where one-third of the Nationalist forces was stationed, I was able (with the assistance of Larry Lutkins, Deputy Director, Chinese Affairs) to submit to Jeff

Parsons that same day our agreed task force recommendations on US countermeasures. These called for a cautious
escalation of US naval and air support operations as necessary to protect Taiwan from a Communist take-over.
Parsons and, subsequently, Robertson approved the recommendations which were forwarded to Dulles. However,
Robertson commented to me that "the US would, of course,
never make first use of nuclear weapons." I found this
remark rather reassuring, coming from one of our leading
hawks.

Dulles, flying down from his vacation retreat on Duck
Island in the St. Lawrence River, immediately called a
meeting in his office. He had obviously read our recommendations but his first concern was legal. What were our
defense obligations towards the offshore islands of Quemoy
and Matsu? What restrictions applied to the involvement of
US forces in their defense?

These small offshore islands were not included in the
Mutual Defense Treaty (between the US and the Republic of
China, or ROC) definition of the treaty area, but a subsequent joint resolution of Congress in January 1955, at the
time of the first Taiwan Straits crisis, authorized the president to employ US armed forces in the protection of not just
Taiwan and the Pescadores but also "related positions and
territories in that area."

Dulles had no difficulty in making a legal case that the
joint resolution covered the off-shore islands in this crisis,
since Beijing in attacking them had announced that its
objective was Taiwan. The president and Congressional
leaders agreed. Establishing rules for the engagement of US
forces was more difficult.

The Quemoy group of islands was so close to mainland
shore batteries that they could be blanketed with enemy
shells, although there was no evidence of any impending

landing operation against those islands. In fact, the shelling occurred immediately before the typhoon season when amphibious operations would have been precarious. It was fairly clear that Beijing did not want to take the islands unless, in so doing, it brought down the government on Taiwan.

Beijing's evident intent was interdiction of the offshore islands to prevent provisions, including food and ammunition, from reaching the defenders. That might wear down the defenders to the point of surrender which in turn might precipitate a collapse of morale on Taiwan and perhaps an eventual takeover from within by the Communists.

The problem therefore came down to one of resupplying the embattled Quemoy group, a task that was beyond the capability of the Nationalist Navy. That force was not only poorly led at that time but had to contend with incessant bombardment of the Quemoy group by Soviet-manufactured artillery. Rough seas and huge tides further complicated the landing of supplies on the islands.

Thus it was arranged that the US Navy would escort Chinese resupply convoys to a point three miles offshore from Quemoy but would not enter Quemoy's territorial waters. Nationalist vessels had to cover the last three miles on their own loaded with supplies including shells for Quemoy's 8-inch howitzers and other guns.

Secretary Dulles, acting under President Eisenhower's instructions, decided against US air operations in the Taiwan Straits and reached agreement with Taibei that US and Nationalist planes would not overfly mainland China. This ruled out air attacks on Communist shore batteries. One important reason for this decision was that the Chinese air force was being used with great restraint, there being no bombing of any Nationalist-held territories. Moreover, there was no way of silencing the batteries short of use of nuclear weapons or extensive air–drops of napalm bombs, actions which President Eisenhower strongly opposed. Our limited rules of engagement also reflected the fact that public opinion in allied countries was highly averse to US military involvement.

Secretary Dulles accordingly was bent on finding some diplomatic course of action that could halt the fighting. He set little store in what the periodic talks in Warsaw could achieve on this issue, although he appreciated that their publicized existence offered relief from criticisms that the US was out of diplomatic contact with Beijing.

Very early on the morning of September 7, 1958, I received a phone call from Dulles, who had evidently had a restless night. He suggested that it might be best for the US to take the issue to the United Nations, since the General Assembly would be reconvening the following week. Dulles mentioned the possibility of having the British and French introduce a resolution in the UN Security Council calling for a UN–supervised cease-fire and neutralization of the offshore islands.

I was strongly opposed to this suggestion. Both Beijing and Taibei would reject it out of hand, and it would impose great strains on our relations with Taibei which in turn might strengthen the case for Beijing to occupy China's seat in the UN. However, I said nothing about all this to Dulles over the phone but replied that he would have our Bureau's reactions as soon as possible.

I forthwith prepared a memorandum, approved by Jeff Parsons and signed by Robertson, pointing out the negative factors entailed in Dulles' suggestion. I recommended that we ask the British and French to introduce a UN resolution welcoming discussion by Washington and Beijing of this issue at Warsaw and urging that the issue be resolved without further resort to force.

Also included in Robertson's memorandum was a suggestion that our side might at some point in the near future take unilateral and unannounced moves such as shifting our regular Taiwan Straits patrols farther away from mainland territorial waters, and/or asking the Nationalists to suspend artillery fire from Quemoy to see whether this invited any reciprocal moves from the Communist side.

However, before any of these strategies could be pursued, our attention had to focus on the immediate, urgent issue of Quemoy running out of supplies. The daily consumption by the 80,000 military and 45,000 civilians on the Quemoy group was estimated at 700 tons and yet, since August 23, only 125 tons had been delivered to Quemoy. This appalling record was ascribed to all the usual reasons: bad weather, tidal conditions, heavy shelling. But it also occurred to some in Washington that Taibei was deliberately holding back, or providing us with false figures, in an effort to involve the US more deeply in defense of the islands.

Our Joint Chiefs of Staff could see no reason why, with the exercise of guts and ingenuity, the Nationalists could not off-load up to 1,000 tons of supplies a day under favorable weather conditions. Admiral Arleigh Burke recommended new ways of delivering supplies, including floating them ashore.

Over the next two weeks there was some improvement in deliveries but not enough to prevent, according to Taibei's reports, an alarming run-down in the availability of food and ammunition on the Quemoys. Soon Taibei reported that only a few days of supplies remained. Cables from our Embassy were full of dire warnings.

At this point Secretary Dulles decided to go to New York to take the issue to the UN along the lines he had suggested over the phone on September 7. However, the very day he left for New York, I received from the CIA a reliable report from Quemoy that its supply situation was nowhere near as desperate as we had been led to believe. There were several weeks of supplies on hand, most of them stored in the extensive network of tunnels on Quemoy.

Robertson asked that I deliver this information in person to the Acting Secretary of State, Christian Herter, who immediately called a meeting in his office. There it was decided that I should go to New York to bring these developments to the attention of Dulles, with a recommendation from Herter that Dulles postpone any UN initiative.

I was met in New York by Ambassador Philip Crowe of USUN who took me to Dulles' suite in the Waldorf. When Dulles heard our reports, he cancelled scheduled meetings with the British and French ambassadors to the UN, returned to Washington, and called a meeting that evening at his house.

The star performer at that meeting was Admiral Burke who was very up-beat on prospects for resupplying the Quemoys. He mentioned for the first time in my hearing the fact that two Landing Ship Docks were about to arrive on station in the Taiwan Straits. These huge vessels could contain dozens of amphibious landing craft, manned by trained Nationalist crews, which could run up on the shores of Quemoy with supplies.

Meanwhile, spirits on Taiwan had been lifted by the deadly effectiveness of several Nationalist fighter aircraft on patrol whose US-provided Sidewinders downed five MIG 17s.

Against this background, Beijing radio announced on October 6 that it was temporarily suspending its bombardment of the offshore islands, emphasizing that its action was taken to spare the lives of Chinese compatriots inhabiting those islands. Our side immediately reciprocated by suspending US convoy activities and modifying our naval patrol routes in the Taiwan Straits. The outlook remained unclear, and when Dulles departed on October 20 for Taibei, via Italy and England, Beijing announced the end of its cease-fire on the alleged grounds that one of our LSDs had intruded into the territorial waters of Quemoy.

On October 25, following the issuance of a joint communique at the conclusion of Dulles' visit to Taibei, Beijing announced its intention to observe a cease-fire on the offshore islands on odd-numbered days. Taibei retaliated by firing on occasional Communist vessels from batteries on Quemoy.

This curious arrangement left each Chinese government with the satisfaction that it was master of the situation, but we had no idea how long this arrangement would continue. Thus, when Dulles returned from Taibei, his first concern was to preserve the relative calm while doing everything he could to get the bulk of Chiang's forces off the offshore islands. On the other hand, we felt we had to be careful in handling this effort, lest sharp open differences between Washington and Taibei tempt Beijing to renew bombardment.

I well recall Secretary Dulles' comments on his return to Washington: "If nothing is done now and a year or so hence the Communists again attack the offshores, it will be extremely difficult for us to give Taibei any military support. Already we have had to strain our relations with Congress and foreign governments to the breaking point. Our experience with the offshores was agonizing enough in 1955. It is worse today. We can't go through this a third time."

Our efforts to effect a drastic reduction in the garrisons on the offshore islands never succeeded. There was an eventual sizeable reduction, but meanwhile we came to appreciate that the Chinese had found a solution, turning their hot war into an endless cold war of propaganda shells, blaring loud speakers, and balloon-delivered leaflets.

Beijing also issued a long series of "serious warnings" to the US every time one of our naval patrols in the Taiwan Straits came within Chinese mainland territorial waters as defined by Beijing, but not by Washington. The serious warnings had nearly reached the thousand mark by the time President Nixon's trip to China was announced in 1971. Thereafter the warnings ceased.

In retrospect, I have often wondered whether Moscow had any hand in Beijing's decision to halt the heavy bombardment of Quemoy. We know that almost all the 580,000 shells fired on the islands were produced in the Soviet Union, and that the first signs of serious Moscow-Beijing differences appeared soon after the Soviets launched Sputnik in 1957, about a year before the 1958 Taiwan Straits crisis. It is possible that Moscow imposed conditions on its support of Beijing's offense. However. we assumed during that crisis that Beijing had Moscow's unqualified support. Moscow said little to suggest otherwise. In fact, Khrushchev warned on several occasions that any use of nuclear weapons would not go unanswered by the USSR. (China exploded its first nuclear weapon in 1964.)

Finally, a few comments about Secretary Dulles' handling of the crisis. I was deeply impressed by his excellent working relations with President Eisenhower and Dulles' associates in State, Defense, and CIA (headed by his brother, Allen). On several occasions, near the conclusion of meetings in his office, Dulles would pick up the secure phone and tell the president of our conclusions and solicit his comments or, where relevant, his approval. Dulles thus made it clear to all present that he was acting under Eisenhower's orders. That, in turn, strengthened Dulles' position with all his associates.

I was also impressed by the way Dulles took charge of the problem, making it his personal responsibility to work out a peaceful solution, losing many hours of sleep in the process. Yet he sought advice from his associates. I recall how Gerard Smith, at that time Director of the State Department's Policy Planning Staff, used to argue almost instinctively against the emerging consensus of several of our meetings. Dulles seemed to welcome the ensuing debate which helped to fine-hone the final decisions.

Diplomatic biographer Sir Harold Nicolson once wrote that the worst kind of diplomatists are zealots, lawyers and missionaries; and the best kind are humane skeptics. In his first years as Secretary of State, John Foster Dulles seemed to fall clearly in the first category. He was a dyed-in-the-wool lawyer with a cold-war missionary zeal. For him, countering Soviet aggressive acts gave rise to a new term in diplomacy: "brinkmanship."

He stonily refused to shake the extended hand of Zhou Enlai at Geneva in 1954 — an insult never forgotten by Zhou. He was also associated in the minds of many of us in the Foreign Service with yielding to Senator McCarthy by dismissing summarily several of our best China specialists whose only "crime" was the accuracy of their reports out of China during World War II.

On substance John Foster Dulles may be remembered by history as one of our most zealous, hard-line Secretaries of State, especially in his dealings with Moscow and Beijing, but from my vantage point, in the last full year of his life, he appeared moderate and reasonable; in short a humane skeptic.

CHAPTER 4

RE-EXAMINING CHINA POLICY

After two stormy years in Korea as Deputy Chief of Mission, I was sent in late 1961 to the relative calm of Hong Kong where the US Consulate General served as our government's eyes and ears covering events inside the vastness of China. The steady stream of refugees from mainland China provided a wealth of information about economic conditions in China, information made available to us through Hong Kong government and private sources. The office also gleaned information from the masses of periodicals, newspapers and letters that reached Hong Kong from all parts of China. We had on our staff 21 people whose sole function was to translate and analyze these written materials.

For me, being head of a large staff comprising some of our most experienced Foreign Service officers in Chinese affairs provided a unique opportunity to listen and to learn. I well remember my first lesson, shortly after my arrival in November 1961, when India seized the Portuguese enclave of Goa. I was alarmed that China would now feel impelled to seize the Portuguese enclave of Macao, some 30 miles from Hong Kong. Since I was also US Consul to Macao, my responsibilities to the several dozen Americans there would seem to involve ordering and assisting in their immediate evacuation. But the head of our Political Section at that time, Dr. Harald Jacobson, recommended otherwise.

In fact, he was completely confident, as was Jack Friedman our Macao expert, that Beijing would not take Macao, for such a seizure would precipitate a collapse of business confidence in Hong Kong and a resulting loss of almost a billion dollars a year which Beijing was making at that time (today it is many times that) through its business ties with

Hong Kong. In other words, Beijing was not about to kill the goose that laid the billion dollar golden egg and which was China's principal source of foreign exchange. So, abiding by Jacobson's recommendation, I wired Washington our conclusions in order to head off likely pressures from the State Department for evacuating all Americans in Macao.

The early 1960's was a period of deepening turmoil and economic disaster in China, due in part to Mao's Great Leap Forward. This was a desperate effort to achieve rapid modernization through self-help, forced-draft industrialization, including a program for building thousands of small furnaces designed to produce steel. Agriculture was badly neglected in the process, resources were squandered and the whole effort collapsed, leaving ruin in its wake.

Analysts in our Consulate General estimated that China's grain production (including potatoes) in 1961 was 160 million tons which was some 30 million tons short of levels required to provide China's teeming population with an adequate diet. Our analysis was based on a variety of sources including comprehensive weather reports and interrogations of thousands of refugees about their daily food consumption. It was challenged by Joe Alsop in his syndicated columns as being too high, but we were vindicated a year later when Zhou Enlai told Lord Montgomery that grain production in China in 1961 was 160 million tons.

I arrived in Hong Kong thinking of China as a powerful threat to its neighbors, purposeful and single-minded in its expansionist design. I soon learned that the Communist regime was floundering, and that its attempts to disperse "surplus" urban dwellers to the farms had deepened discontent among urban and rural dwellers alike. The touted public discipline of China was decaying, as evidenced by signs of growing corruption, bureaucratic indifference, and general laxity that permeated even the youth and armed forces. The capacity of the Chinese people to endure privations was legendary, and China's ability to exploit troubles along its borders was unchanged, but it was clearly not the fearsome dragon conjured up in the minds of many Americans.

More importantly, China no longer had an ally in Russia. The Sino-Soviet rift that made its first appearance after the Sputnik launching in 1957 had, by early 1962, reached the stage where it was beyond the ability of our translators to find expressions in English equal to Beijing's scatological denunciations of the Kremlin.

Many of us in the Consulate General felt that we over-advertised our concern and worry over China's aggressive power, and that this invited bluster, threat and intervention from the Communist side. We thought we would be in a more competitive position psychologically if we appeared to be less harried and worried over Beijing's threats. We would also stand to gain greater international support for our position if our views were expressed in more objective, factual and unemotional terms.

At the same time, we fully supported continuation of a US policy of firmness in the defense of "free world" positions and maintaining adequate capabilities for pursuing that policy successfully. We did weigh in strongly against unnecessary provocations of Communist China, such as the occasional sabotage operations being conducted by the Chinese Nationalists from Taiwan against targets on the China mainland. These operations were not only fruitless, but they damaged Taibei's international standing. Moreover, such operations, to the extent that they involved Hong Kong, could endanger Hong Kong and were deeply resented by its government.

A golden opportunity to present these views to key figures in the new Kennedy Administration occurred in the Spring of 1962 at a meeting of all our East Asia/Australasia

Chiefs of Missions at Baguio in the Philippines. This meeting was presided over by Under Secretary of State Chester Bowles and Assistant Secretary Averell Harriman, both of whom reacted favorably to my presentation of how we in the Consulate General evaluated the scene in China and its implications for US policy. This established a useful meeting of minds between our Consulate General and policy makers in Washington.

One of the effects of economic set-backs in China was to increase the flow of refugees to Hong Kong. In 1962 a severe drought in South China coincided with a temporary break-down in the ability (or willingness) of PRC officials in Guangdung to restrain the flow of refugees, many of whom were young people who had been forced out of the cities to live in rural areas. It appeared for a while that the Chinese authorities had decided to allow them to flee to Hong Kong, if only to ease pressures on food supplies and lessen problems for China created by these disgruntled elements.

The number of refugees got so large that the Hong Kong Government constructed massive barriers of concertina wire all along its land frontier with China. But every night the refugees merely threw planks across the wire and swarmed in, only to be rounded up by the Hong Kong garrisons and forced back into China (although many eluded the police and managed to get into the city).

At first the Hong Kong Government forbore from making any representations to Beijing on this appalling situation, evidently fearing that Beijing would reject Hong Kong's protests and Hong Kong would then have to live with the results. Besides, Hong Kong had only the status of a colony, and had to deal with Beijing through London. Meanwhile, I was receiving expressions of concern from the State Department which was torn between wanting Hong Kong to accept refugees as a matter of principle, and a sober awareness of how such huge numbers of refugees could turn Hong Kong into another Gaza Strip.

Washington was quietly urging London to take up the issue with Beijing, but Hong Kong recommended otherwise to London. As I learned from Murray Maclehose, at that time political adviser to Hong Kong's Governor Black (later Maclehose became one of Hong Kong's most effective governors), Hong Kong had reason to believe that Beijing would soon, **on its own initiative**, restore controls along the Hong Kong frontier because of the bad press China was receiving world-wide, with millions of Chinese seeking to escape China. Governor Black's policy proved successful, but not before 170,000 Chinese refugees had succeeded in sneaking permanently into over-crowded Hong Kong in the period of one month.

Many practical issues had to be addressed on a day-to-day basis between Hong Kong and Canton relating to trade, transportation, migration, water supply and finances. All these issues were handled by Hong Kong officials with low-key common sense in a way best designed to avoid affronting its giant neighbor.

There was recognition on both sides of the compelling material advantages in peaceful coexistence, even though Hong Kong's spectacular economic success story on the very doorstep of backward China was, in itself, an affront. Hong Kong was at pains to pay for the water piped in from China (about 20 to 25 percent of Hong Kong's needs), even though China offered to provide this water free of charge. Hong Kong wanted to ensure that China had a material stake in continuing the water supply in order to minimize chances that China might cut it off at some point in order to impose pressures on Hong Kong for whatever reason. To me, this was convincing evidence that constructive relations with revolutionary Communist China were possible for the

United States provided Beijing came to see compelling material and strategic reasons for such relations.

Not only were we mighty busy those days with refugees, consular work, textile negotiations, and countless visitors, but I had to meet, wine and dine the many Congressional delegations who were attracted to Hong Kong. We also put on some good briefings for VIPs on developments in China, including our policy conclusions. We found that almost all of the Congressional visitors shared our views on US policy implications.

During my 21 months in Hong Kong, I had lengthy discussions with my deputy, John Lacey, who was not only an excellent administrator and negotiator on US–Hong Kong textile issues, but whose views on China policy were practical and forward–looking. We drafted a message to Washington in February 1963, in which we posed the question whether we were missing any opportunities to abet forces in China that might be seeking pragmatic changes.

We then recommended seven specific ways for enhancing our capacity to influence attitudes in China in a desirable direction, though admitting that even their combined effect might be very slight in the immediate future.

The closing of our airgram was prophetic: "Distasteful as it has been for Mao and his cohorts, they have already been obliged to make some concessions basically in conflict with their ideologies. When the hard–line doctrinaires no longer dominate the scene, the influence of pragmatism may well intensify. Our present containment policy should be aimed at abetting that process. . . . All this argues for a policy of continued restraint which allows and encourages change with mainland China. . . ."

We also urged a review of regulations preventing our newsmen and scholars from visiting China. Even if they would not be admitted by the Chinese, a relaxed US policy would make it clear that it was not our fault that China was closed to much of the outside world.

Civility Amid Obstacles

By mid–1963, the Kennedy administration was ready to take a fresh look at China policy. Roger Hilsman, Assistant Secretary for the Far East, was a personal friend of the president. Transferred from Hong Kong to be Hilsman's principal deputy, I was assigned to concentrate on China policy review with Lindsey Grant, a brilliant young China specialist as my assistant, with generous help from Jim Thomson (on detail from Harvard) and Joe Neubert, Hilsman's aide. We held periodic meetings with leading American scholars knowledgeable about East Asia, a practice our Bureau was to continue for many years.

Our first move was to reorganize the Bureau to give greater attention to Communist Asia. At that time we had only two officers (out of the hundred or more in our Bureau) who were devoting their full time to this critical subject. None of our officers was giving much time and attention to North Korea, North Vietnam and Mongolia, even though Communist Asia comprised two-thirds of the land area and population of East Asia. We accordingly established a new office called ACA (Asian Communist Affairs) whose four officers were responsible for mainland China, North Korea, North Vietnam and Mongolia.

We also managed to have two able Foreign Service officers sent to Moscow for several years of instruction in Mongolian, but our recommendation for establishing US relations with Mongolia, accepted in principle by key officials like Governor Harriman, encountered years of delay in implementation.

US diplomatic contacts with Beijing at that time were confined to the ambassadorial level talks at Warsaw which had been going on intermittently ever since they started at Vienna in 1954. These talks achieved only limited results, but they ultimately succeeded in bringing about the release of all but two of the Americans held in mainland China. They further provided a forum for clarifying our position on certain issues, especially a peaceful resolution of the Taiwan problem. Above all, they enabled the US government to say quite truthfully that we had, in Warsaw, more official exchanges than most governments which had recognized Beijing.

Maoist doctrine sharply circumscribed what new courses of action were open to us, and our ability to influence events inside China was almost nil. But, over the longer range, opening China's contacts with the outside world could have more of a salutary impact than a negative one, and it seemed important that we at least demonstrate to the world that Communist China's isolation from the world was self-imposed and not the result of US policies to contain Chinese Communism.

This was not easy to do. The United States had taken the lead year after year in trying to keep Beijing out of the United Nations. We had also taken the lead in establishing controls designed to prevent any strategic materials from reaching Communist China from the Free World. Carrying out these policies involved constant pressures on friends and allies, contributing to a rather widespread impression that it was US policy to cut off Chinese contacts with the outside world.

This, in fact, was not our policy. In 1959, the US at long last allowed 25 selected newsmen to have restrictions removed from their passports to permit them to visit mainland China. For months they sat it out in Hong Kong seeking Chinese visas. None was granted. In 1962, we announced that we would give favorable attention to any bona fide Chinese request for purchase of US wheat or other grains. Beijing never responded.

The first substantive policy change we recommended to Hilsman, on October 10, 1963, was that our government should seek to lift all US travel restrictions. This would be a world-wide change in travel policy, and would not be presented as an initiative to "liberalize" US policy towards Communist China (or other Communist countries) for this would be immediately interpreted as a softening of the US position. Nor did we base our efforts to broaden contacts on the assumption that they would probably be rejected. We did these things because of their intrinsic merit —to break down barriers between nations and peoples, to broaden understanding. Privately, we could explain that our changes in travel policy were designed to show our strength and confidence at a time when China was fearful of outside contacts because of the ferment brewing behind the curtain.

Recommendations for liberalizing rules governing travel of Americans was not a new idea. The Legal Adviser and the Assistant Secretary for Security and Consular Affairs had already favored the idea when it was first advanced in a more modified form by Hilsman in June, 1963. However, Under Secretary of State Averell Harriman believed that a formal modification of existing regulations would stir up too much adverse attention. He recommended that State quietly adopt a more permissive policy governing exceptions to the current travel ban, and that is where the matter stood when Lindsey Grant and I became involved.

All we could do at that stage was to press for liberalizing exceptions. We succeeded in having US passports validated for travel to mainland China for three categories: representatives of accredited news gathering organizations; family members of Americans in prison in China; and, in 1965, US doctors and public health experts.

Our Bureau was similarly frustrated in its efforts to ease restrictions on US trade with China, starting with putting medicines and foodstuffs on general license. We did not think China would make any US purchases in the light of its "buy anything but American" policy, but it would create a useful precedent if at some future date the Chinese wished to move away from their present frozen hostility.

In one important respect we succeeded. That was in recommending that our public treatment of Communist China be more moderate, civil, and factual. This was reflected in a key speech made by Roger Hilsman at San Francisco on December 13, 1963. At first Secretary Rusk was annoyed over Hilsman's failure to get top-level clearance, but public and press reactions to the Hilsman speech were so overwhelmingly favorable that the Secretary reflected the same points of view in a speech he made on February 25, 1964. Meanwhile, we sent guidance to our embassies on the importance of making it clear that it was the Chinese Communists, not the US, who were bellicose and unwilling to accept a world of diversity, as well as the importance of US officials speaking more coolly, factually and civilly about Communist China.

In retrospect there is little question that our efforts in 1963 to liberalize US policy toward mainland China failed due to major events on the other side of the Pacific.

Even if President Kennedy had served out his full term in office, it is unlikely that any major revisions in existing China policy would have occurred during that term. It is true that his thinking about China parallelled that of his associates like Harriman, Bowles, Ball and Hilsman. On the other hand, he was being drawn more and more into the vortex of Vietnam, and Vietnam was to claim the full attention of President Johnson. With Beijing evidently giving strong support to Hanoi (despite long-standing Sino-Vietnamese antipathies), it seemed all the more unlikely that any US administration would or could make substantive changes in China policy.

More importantly, in 1964 Mao Zedong and his entourage of ideologues were intent on revising the across-the-board liberalization of the early 1960's. The Socialist Education Campaign (a precursor to the Cultural Revolution which was launched in late 1965) sought to carry out class education of youth, eliminate bourgeois influence, and stamp out "the spontaneous tendency to capitalism." This coincided with China's successful nuclear weapons test in 1964. The opportunities we saw in 1962 and 1963 for improving long-term US-Chinese relations were now fast disappearing. US-China relations were about to enter the deep freeze of the Cultural Revolution, which lasted until the early 1970's.

William Bundy succeeded Roger Hilsman early in 1964. Intellectually gifted and with many years of experience in higher levels of CIA and the Defense Department, he was deeply involved in our many problems in Southeast Asia but was also keenly concerned with great-power inter-relationships.

He was receptive to a proposal made by Harald Jacobson, the Country Director, for establishing, with Secretary Rusk's approval, an Advisory Panel on China, including such leading scholars concerned with China as Lucien Pye, Robert Scalapino, and Doak Barnett.

In a well-publicized speech I made at Princeton University in May 1965, I said: "Peiping's policy toward the US is very simple. It is one of avowed hostility. It does not allow even for the working out of lesser problems in our relations . . . . As a Chinese Communist document puts it, 'we do not wish to settle our disputes with the United States on a piecemeal basis; else we will undermine the revolutionary fervor of our own people. **When the time comes for a settlement, it will be done all at once.'** " (Emphasis added.)

I did not realize at the time how prophetic that last sentence would prove to be: China in seven years would decide it was time for a settlement with the US "all at once" in the form of the Shanghai Communique of February 1972.

A major obstacle in US-China relations of 1964–65 was the war in Vietnam. As I wrote in May 1965, "The Chinese Communists see the US as caught on the flypaper of South Vietnam, and they do not want to see us wriggle off through negotiations and settlement." On the other hand, Beijing was concerned that the Soviets were moving into Southeast Asia, by virtue of close ties with Hanoi, in a way designed to deprive China of the fruits of victory. There were numerous economic and military reasons why China did not intervene more directly against the US in Vietnam, but the underlying reality was the long historic roots of enmity and antipathy between China and Vietnam.

As usual our Consulate General in Hong Kong had the clearest view of trends in Communist Asia. On returning in late 1964 from a meeting with Consul General Ed Rice and his Hong Kong staff, I reported their view that Hanoi was definitely opposed to any large presence of Chinese Communists in North Vietnam. "In fact a threat of their coming in might be a major inducement for Hanoi to come to terms with us." The Consulate General also believed that "our bombings of the north are making the North Vietnamese even more tough and resistant, and the only merit of the bombings is temporarily to bolster morale in the south." The Consulate General foresaw little likelihood of any real settlement of the war being reached at the conference table.

Beijing, in fact, was hoping for major gains elsewhere, and I was to be in the middle of it.

CHAPTER 5

ABORTED COUP IN INDONESIA – THE CHINA CONNECTION

When I was assigned to Indonesia in June 1965, *The Washington Post* editorially deplored the sending of an American Ambassador to Indonesia because of President Sukarno's destructive policies and because "Green's departure would remove from Washington the one policy man in the administration charged with taking a long-range look at US relations with Communist China." My four years in Indonesia nevertheless turned out to have a lot more to do with China and China policy than anyone could have foreseen. It was also in Indonesia in April 1967 that I first met Mr. Nixon (a New York lawyer at that time) and engaged in the first of several conversations I had with him over the next several years on US-China policy.

At the time of my appointment to Indonesia, the US was deeply preoccupied with Vietnam. Washington never did focus on Indonesia as a potential Communist country, even though it was headed in that direction.

It is true that President Sukarno's words infuriated Washington. So too did Indonesia's armed confrontation with Malaysia, the attacks on foreign missions in Jakarta, plans for expropriating foreign companies including Caltex and Goodyear, Sukarno's raging at my predecessor Howard Jones "to Hell with your aid," Indonesia's walking out of the United Nations and its agencies, and its increasing alignment with China and other forces hostile to the United States. But these were considered by many in Washington to be the antics of a vainglorious man — a dangerous man, to be sure, but not a very serious man, rather one who sought the world spotlight.

The Chinese Communists took Sukarno far more seriously than we did. They recognized Indonesia to be a significant potential Communist state and ally. By 1965, the Indonesian Communist Party (PKI) had become the largest and most influential political force in Indonesia, as well as being by far the largest Communist party outside the USSR and China. The PKI favored Sukarno, and he them. On one occasion when Sukarno was referring to PKI leader Aidit, he shouted before the crowds at Senayen arena: "I wish I had a thousand Aidits." Sukarno's drift toward and affinity for Communism also related to Indonesia's imminent economic collapse due to inept policies, extravagance and mismanagement.

Even though Sukarno's avowed goal was to establish a NASAKOM government (acronym for Nationalism, Religion, and Communism), Washington continued to see Indonesia as a fractious element, not as a potential hostile force in the constellation of world power.

By late 1964, Sino-Indonesian relations were converging both at the level of the two Communist parties and at the governmental level. The Communist Party of Indonesia had sided completely with the Chinese Party in the latter's view that revolutionary prospects were highly favorable in the former colonial world (especially Southeast Asia) and that leadership of the world revolutionary movement was passing from Soviet to Asian hands. Differences with the Soviets were also reflected in positions taken by Sukarno's government, even though it continued to receive considerable Soviet aid, especially military hardware.

At the governmental level, Sukarno announced to the million or more people crowding Merdeka Square on August 17, 1965, (Indonesia's national day), the formation of the Beijing-Jakarta-Pyongyang-Hanoi axis. This announcement was made in the presence of top officials of Communist Asia, including Chinese Foreign Minister Chen Yi. I realized in advance of this occasion that it would be used by Sukarno to blast the United States in such a way that normal diplomatic practice would require my walking out of the pavilion where all the diplomatic corps was seated. But I had already decided, with Washington's telegraphic approval, not to give Sukarno that satisfaction, so I stoically sat it out, with press cameras trained on me.

During Indonesia's confrontation with Malaysia and the U.K., Beijing was urging Sukarno to accelerate the radicalization of his policies and use the confrontation as a means of establishing and arming a "Fifth Force," largely composed of Communist organizations, to be a counteragent to the Indonesian Army. All these developments polarized differences between the Indonesian Army on the one hand and the Communists (PKI), supported by Sukarno, on the other.

Sukarno became seriously ill in late August 1965, which immediately raised fears among the Communists (and probably the Air Force which was led by leftists) that, should Sukarno die, the Army would move in and crush the Communists. It was in that setting that the PKI planned a coup against the Army, almost certainly with the knowledge of the Chinese Communists and possibly with their approval.

On the night of September 30–October 1, 1965, the PKI hunted down and killed six of Indonesia's eight top army generals and seized control of Jakarta. It announced over the radio that the "September 30 movement" had taken control of the government in order to forestall a CIA-supported plot by the Generals to oust Sukarno and establish a military government. (In fact there was no CIA or other US foreknowledge of the Communist coup or of any General's plot to oust Sukarno. Army generals deplored Sukarno's Communist leanings but they would not challenge him or refuse to take orders.)

However, the Indonesian Army moved quickly against the Communist coup and suppressed it within a day or two. This left Sukarno weakened and suspect, and he eventually was replaced by Suharto, one of the two ranking surviving generals. Meanwhile, the PKI was shattered and tens of thousands of suspected Communists were assassinated by anti-Communist forces, mostly in the rural areas of Java and Bali. A disproportionate number of those killed were of Chinese ethnic origin, probably because Indonesians had a racial bias against the three million Sino-Indonesians, who were resented because of their control of moneylending and retail trade.

The failure of the coup attempt was a devastating setback for Communist China, whose role therein was suspect. Twelve separate Indonesian delegations were in China at the time of the coup, including delegations headed by the Deputy Prime Minister, the Head of the Air Force, and the Head of the National Defense Institute. There was also a large PKI delegation which, unlike previous PKI delegations sent to China, did not include any of its top level officers. The latter evidently remained in Indonesia because of the critical events about to unfold.

Most significant of all was the evidence, subsequently received, that the Chinese knew what to expect. According to Robert Martens, our Embassy's expert on Sino-Soviet affairs who has spent many months researching the events of September 30-October 1, 1965, the Chinese leadership at that critical moment showed itself to be remarkably well informed. The Chinese reportedly had a complete list of the assassinated generals by 11 a.m. October 1, which was 5 hours before this information was announced in Jakarta. The list included the name of General Nasution (who had escaped assassination but whose inclusion suggests that the Chinese had an advance PKI target list.)

October 1 was also China's national day and it was apparently to be not only a day of celebration of past victory on the China mainland but also of a far-reaching new victory that would add the world's fifth most populous nation to the Asian Communist Camp.

The Communist coup failure in Indonesia shattered China's alliance with Indonesia and its hopes for a radical tide sweeping over all the developing world, led by China. The famous Lin Biao speech of September 1965 had boasted that the world countryside was surrounding the world city, which meant an Asian Communist encirclement of the US and USSR. A successful Sino–Indonesian alliance would also have created a giant pincer within which Vietnam would be caught.

Instead, Indonesia under General Suharto crushed the PKI, gradually removed Sukarno, established a New Order in Indonesia with close ties with its neighbors and the West, rejoined the United Nations, and, along with Thailand, took the lead in forming the Association of Southeast Asian Nations (ASEAN). Indonesia also severed diplomatic ties with China.

The extraordinary reversal in Indonesia in the period 1965–67 never received the international attention it deserved, especially in the United States, which was so totally pre-occupied with Vietnam. Our Embassy in Jakarta was also at pains to warn Washington against taking any credit for what happened in Indonesia. The aborted coup was entirely an Indonesian performance in which we played no role whatsoever. Any US government efforts to take credit for the reversal would only have bolstered the false Communist claims that the US was involved in a plot to remove Sukarno and the PKI. A full account of these events appears in my book, *Indonesia in Crisis and Transformation*, Compass Press, Washington, DC, 1991.

The aborted Communist coup in the short run seems to have spurred China's self-destructive course toward the Great Proletarian Cultural Revolution, putting US–Chinese relations in an even deeper freeze. In the long run, these setbacks and excesses strengthened the hand of the pragmatists led by Zhou Enlai.

Ambassador Green at funeral for six Indonesian Army generals slain by the Communists. In reprisal the Army crushed the PKI and ousted President Sukarno, their protector: both were critical setbacks for China. (October 1965).

Mr. Richard Nixon was our house guest for two days in April 1967. When we called on President Suharto, Foreign Minister Malik and others, Mr. Nixon took down notes on key points they made. After dinner that night, he and I had a long conversation on events in Indonesia and the rest of East Asia, especially China. Our conversation was tape-recorded by Mr. Nixon. When I asked him what he did with all these notes and tapes, he replied that he had them tran-scribed, filed and cross-filed for later reference.

For example, I told him that the rate of inflation in Indonesia in 1965 was 635%. He included that obscure fact in his Guam Doctrine press interview on July 27, 1969. His tape recording was, of course, to lead to his eventual undo-ing, but I remember him as the best informed on foreign affairs of all the luminaries who visited Jakarta during my four years there.

In an article he wrote for *Foreign Affairs* (October 1967 issue), Mr. Nixon described the 1965-66 turnaround in Indonesia as "an extraordinarily promising transformation" in a key country that was "by far the richest prize in the Southeast Asian area." Although most of the article stressed the need for a new regional grouping to deal with "the Chinese threat," he concluded that "any American policy toward Asia must come to grips with the reality of Chi-na...Taking the long view, we simply cannot afford to leave China forever outside the family of nations. . . to live in an angry isolation."

During my last few months as Ambassador to Indonesia, I was assigned to serve concurrently on the US negotiating team to the Paris talks on Vietnam. In March 1969 I was appointed Assistant Secretary of State for East Asia and the Pacific, a position I held for four years. This brought me back into the center of US-China relations, working for a president who was destined to make those relations his greatest foreign policy triumph.

Dinner for Mr. Richard Nixon during his visit to Jakarta. On Lisa Green's right is Foreign Minister Adam Malik (April 1967).

The great turnaround in Indonesia explained by Ambassador Green to the Cabinet at the request of President Johnson (October 1967).

President Chiang Kai-shek greeting Assistant Secretary-designate Green and Mrs. Green at presidential residence, Taibei; with Ambassador and Mrs. Walter McConaughy. (April 1969).

President Nixon confers with East Asian chiefs of mission and CINC-PAC in Bangkok, with Sino-Soviet and Vietnam relations major topics: On president's right are Ambassadors Ellsworth Bunker (Vietnam) and Carol Laise (Nepal); on his left, Leonard Unger (Thailand), Marshall Green, Arthur Hummel Jr. (Burma), and Mac Godley (Laos). July 1969.

CHAPTER 6

THE MAOIST INSURGENCY IN THAILAND

by William N. Stokes

After its disappointment with the coup in Indonesia, China retained another, more direct hope for gaining influence, this time by fomenting insurrection in Thailand, where victory could open the whole of Southeast Asia to Chinese Communist influence.

Almost unnoticed in the publicity given the war in Vietnam, a Maoist-inspired insurgency was launched in the Thai northeast. There Mao sought to extend Chinese influence by inexpensive and indirect military means, more like his unconventional successes, first against the Japanese and later in the Chinese civil war. Insurgents were open enough about their Chinese inspiration: they wore Mao buttons, were led by Chinese-trained cadres and were supported by radio broadcasts in Thai from South China.

I came to this "silent struggle" by way of the Pentagon, where I acquired invaluable credentials. In 1965 I was loaned to Air Force GHQ, advising on strategic air basing in Southeast Asia, then in full course of expansion. I presented a paper to the Joint Chiefs on the uses of aviation in countering insurgency, a work later cited in a Distinguished Civilian Service Award by the Air Force Secretary, Harold Brown. A period of temporary duty in Northeast Thailand involved overseeing the replacement of US personnel in helicopter supply missions by newly-trained Thai pilots and mechanics. This work brought me to the attention of Graham Martin, our ambassador in Bangkok, who asked me to join his staff in dealing with the insurgency.

A fundamental issue for both the State and Defense Departments was whether the insurgency in Thailand was **primarily** "war," and thus subject to military strategy and direction, or "nation building," which called for a balance of social and economic development, political reform, and security measures, more amenable to civilian leadership. In Thailand, the latter view prevailed, marked by the appointment as Ambassador of Leonard Unger, who confirmed me as his Mission Coordinator in Bangkok. As such I was responsible for assisting Peer de Silva of CIA and his successor, Dr. George Tanham of RAND, in advising the Thai Government on means of countering the insurgency. For this purpose, Tanham and I led a large US inter-agency staff coordinating civil, police and military programs.

The radical difference of American approach in Vietnam and Thailand was spelled out in guidelines developed by Tanham and myself. American advisors and personnel were strictly forbidden to participate or even advise in field operations while the operations were in progress. This policy concentrated responsibility on the Thai Government for dealing with its insurgency problem, thereby avoiding the operational American involvement so tragically manifest in Vietnam at the time. This approach later was incorporated in the Nixon Guam Doctrine.

When Tanham resigned, I succeeded him. The Air Force concurred in my appointment, based on my experience with the Air Staff. This was the first appointment of a Foreign Service officer to leadership of a national inter-agency program to counter insurgency. The post had been aggressively sought by the US Army, as the best solution for a "military problem." State argued that the insurgency in Thailand was fundamentally different from that in Vietnam, and required a diametrically different response. Marshall

Green, who was then Assistant Secretary, held firmly to this position and prevailed because of Nixon's Guam Doctrine.

There was plenty of opposition. Several major initiatives within the US Army and the CIA to reverse this policy, based on cries of alarm about the insurgency threat, were turned aside when I appealed to the ambassador. He was strongly backed by the State Department and CINCPAC, who caused the removal of a US Army commanding general in Thailand who had violated policy by advising the Thai Army to request B-52 bombardment of Thai insurgent base areas.

Threats to US Bases

Much was at stake, because the 40,000 American airmen at six major bases in Thailand, conducting the air war in Vietnam and Laos, were located in the heart of the Chinese-inspired insurgency in the Northeast. Ambassador Unger insisted on applying the "Thais are responsible" counter-insurgency strategy also to defending the US air bases from Vietnamese retaliation, and empowered me to develop and apply specific rules of engagement.

When Vietnamese cross-border raids on the US Air Force bases in Thailand began, US personnel were limited by our strategy to defense from within base perimeters. Urgent Pentagon offers of a regimental combat team were declined. Ambassador Unger instructed US commanders and me to meet with Thai leaders to underscore US reliance on Thai readiness and initiative. This meeting led to our supplying communications equipment to the Thai police and civil administrators along the border to make possible early warning of attacks, thereby assuring readiness of US base defenses.

The policy of non-intervention proved successful. With timely advance warning from Thai villagers through Thai civil channels, five North Vietnamese cross-border attacks on major US airbases were repelled on base perimeters, without American casualties or serious damage, in sharp contrast to the severe losses often suffered at US bases in Vietnam.

The gains in Thai self-confidence from our restricting US operations in this manner also had important long term effects. Later, when US forces withdrew, Thailand was able to defend itself against Vietnam even when Vietnamese forces occupied Cambodia and neared the approaches to Bangkok. So much for the "domino theory," that Communism would be irresistible in Southeast Asia without US operational involvement.

The Maoist Insurgency

Parallel gains against the insurgency were realized. In face of the growing Thai investment in rural infra-structure, a more responsive rural administration and a security presence more sensitive to needs of the rural population, the Maoist political and social appeal, and thus the insurgency's hopes of recruitment and wider popular influence, eroded steadily. These measures were developed with US interagency assistance in materiel and institutional development for the affected areas, which historically had been neglected and exploited by officials from Bangkok. The Chinese-inspired insurgency eventually collapsed under this combined program, despite few if any military reverses.

Thus, by unobtrusively encouraging Thai leadership and initiative while refusing to involve US personnel in any operational role, we made what may be termed "Unhistory." We forestalled international military escalation and induced a quiet end to subversive campaigns. In this manner, the force of Thai nationalism was retained by the central administration. This approach, though it seemed less certain of success at the time, proved to be far more efficacious and less expensive than primary reliance on military force and direct action by the US as applied in Vietnam. Today Thailand has grown, largely through the experience of countering its insurgency, from a city–state in outlook to a nation–state, effective with regional allies in assuring collective self–defense. In 1971 came a sea change in China. Lin Biao, Mao's designated successor, who had advocated exporting revolution and opposed an opening with the US was himself "exported" by Zhou Enlai.

(Anticipating briefly the story to follow in order to complete the Thai picture, by 1972 Chinese leaders recognized that the Maoist insurgency in Thailand had no future. During the Nixon discussions in China, Marshall Green sought indications that Chinese support for the insurgency would be curtailed. He gathered that the flow of weaponry and training would cease, but that propaganda broadcasts would continue (thus avoiding public admission of defeat). Given the Thai success by that time in reducing internal vulnerabilities to subversion, the Chinese offer was a welcome acceptance of reality, as well as a harbinger of normalization of relations with Thailand that was soon to transpire.)

The failure of Maoist guerilla strategy in Thailand played a peripheral role in discrediting Mao and the Cultural Revolution and in the rise of a more cooperative Chinese foreign policy. Indeed, the change toward cooperation with the United States was led by the spiritual heirs of those who had stood for such an approach in Shenyang thirty years before.

The Thai shore of the Mekong at Nakhon Phanom —the epicenter of the Maoist insurgency and basing for US airstrikes over the Ho Chi Minh Trail. Laos and the Trail are in the background. Thai Lt. Gen. Saiyud Kherdphol, leader of the combined Thai counter-insurgency effort, with Stokes is greeted by the district officer. (October 1971).

Senior counter-insurgency coordinating group, US Mission, Bangkok: l/r SA Lewis Lapham; USIA Director Lou Schmidt; SA/CI George Tanham; AID Director Rey Hill; ARPA Director Phil Worschel; Maj. Gen. Jack Flagstaff, US Army and Stokes. (December 1971).

It was a shift I had long hoped for. In early 1964, in a presentation to the Industrial College of the Armed Forces entitled "The Future Between America and China" I analyzed US experiences in Northeast China and reviewed the misunderstandings and factional divisions on both sides of the Pacific and concluded that the then-current hostility reflected more transitory than fundamental influences. Mutual long-term benefits from a cooperative relationship were outlined:

"The Chinese people are justly famous for pragmatic realism in economic matters. This quality asserted itself in skepticism at Mao's doctrinaire course, already compromised by the gross blunders of the Great Leap Forward and the commune system. Many Chinese managers must realize that China's economy can be developed only by opening broad trade and joint ventures with the dollar area, after reducing tensions and military expenditure.

". . . The best field for achievement of China's rights and hopes lies within the world order that Mao is now defying. Indeed, Mao's personal rule has outlived its usefulness for China . . . although the succession to Mao can only be determined **within** the Chinese political structure.

"Is it fanciful to compare the present tragic state of Sino -American relations with the late Stalinist era of our dealings with Russia? The determined yet prudent containment of Stalin's ambitions, against the counsels of preventive war, seems to have fostered revulsion against Stalinism in Russian society. There is reason, in time, to expect a similar development in China."

The State Department approved broadcast of my main points by the Voice of America to the mainland in Mandarin. Chinese Party officials in China read it in their confidential summary of world news, and some may have accepted it as intended: an early overture for the peace that would be realized eight years later.

The hill tribes of north Thailand, linked by their frequent migration to relatives in Laos and China, were a key element in border defense. Ambassador Leonard Unger, William Stokes, SA "Red" Janssen, AID Director Harold Parsons, and Mac Prosser (AID delegate to the joint counter-insurgency staff) are led in a visit to a hill tribe by the Thai district officer. (April 1968).

CHAPTER 7

OMENS OF CHANGE

by Marshall Green

Three months service on our Paris delegation gave me opportunities to meet President Nixon, Secretary Rogers and National Security Adviser Kissinger (for the first time). When I met the president in Paris he recalled our talks in Jakarta two years earlier, calling me "low-profile Green" because of the emphasis I had placed on maintaining a low-profile American presence in Indonesia. I had also given a publicized talk to the American Chamber of Commerce in Paris advocating more "Modesty, Mutuality and Multilateralism" in the conduct of US foreign policy.

Shortly thereafter I replaced my old friend and Yale classmate, Bill Bundy, as Assistant Secretary for East Asian Affairs. But first I went to say farewell to friends in Indonesia, especially Suharto and Malik, figuring that such a trip would give me an opportunity to visit other countries in my area of responsibility, and that, as the first emissary of the Nixon Administration to be sent to that area, I should be in a position in conversations with Asian leaders to reflect accurately the views of our new president.

I accordingly requested a private White House meeting with the president and co-drafted with Ambassador Win Brown, my deputy, and with Bob Barnett, deputy for economic affairs (who had also been of invaluable assistance to me in Indonesia), an informal three-page memorandum setting forth what the three of us regarded as President Nixon's viewpoints on key policy issues of interest to Asian leaders. This memorandum was based on things the president had said or written, or which we believed reflected his viewpoint (or should).

When we met, President Nixon approved my use of the memorandum. Just as he did so, in walked Henry Kissinger who was visibly annoyed by my having by-passed him in getting in to the Oval Office.

Upon my return from the ensuing Asian trip in April 1969 that included meetings with many top leaders, I included in my written report to Secretary Rogers a statement that there seemed to be a universally-held judgment among all the Asian leaders I met that China had never been in such a negative, truculent mood as it was at that time. Asian leaders felt that any hope of progress in establishing a constructive dialogue with China was out of the question until the Cultural Revolution subsided. A main theme related to the need for downsizing the American official presence in East Asia, especially by eliminating large numbers of US military contract personnel.

President Nixon pencilled "this is great" on my trip report when Secretary Rogers sent him an abbreviated copy, and the president directed Kissinger to circulate copies of the report to top officials in our foreign policy community.

The president showed continuing interest in achieving a breakthrough in our frozen relationship with the PRC. I recall that on our return from his meeting with Vietnamese President Thieu at Midway Island in early June 1969, President Nixon invited me to his cabin on Air Force One where for nearly two hours we discussed China and other Asian issues. The president was interested in the history of our efforts to achieve some thaw in US-China relations.

I also told the president about my recent meeting with the old Gimo on Taiwan, where President Chiang seemed out of touch with reality, at least on the Sino-Soviet dispute, which he regarded as a collusive effort by China and Russia to delude and divide the West.

The president stressed that we should try to remove unnecessary irritants in our relations with China, but that we should not do this in a way that would unnecessarily provoke the USSR, or that was designed to exploit Sino-Soviet differences.

Shortly thereafter, in late July 1969, I accompanied President Nixon on the Pacific-East Asian phase of his round-the-world trip. Together with Bob Barnett I had prepared the "scope-paper" for that phase of his trip. Much of its content was reflected in Nixon's famous press backgrounder on July 25 at Guam, his first stop. In the scope-paper I had emphasized the great economic up-surge of East Asian countries and the growing ability of most East Asian countries to assume greater burdens for their own defense. I also said that our general position in East Asia should not be one of trying to solve East Asia's problems but rather of helping East Asia's problem-solvers.

The president made several references to China in his backgrounder, including modifications he hoped to see in permitting travel of Americans to China and allowing limited tourist purchase of Chinese products.

What undoubtedly interested Beijing most was the president's thesis that:

(a) the US would stand by its treaty commitments,

(b) the US would provide a shield if a nuclear power threatened any US ally **or** a nation whose survival we considered vital to our own survival, and

(c) the US looked to the country threatened to assume the primary responsibility for providing the manpower for its own defense.

The president also made it clear that the US should learn from the experience of Vietnam and not get caught in another comparable situation of "creeping involvement." He said, "I want to be sure that our policies in the future, all over the world . . . reduce American involvement."

In retrospect it is fair to assume that these statements of America's role in the world helped set the stage for the Chinese–American rapprochement that was to occur within two years of the Nixon Doctrine.

During 1969 the Administration made a number of statements and moves, beyond those already mentioned, to create a better climate in US Chinese relations. We publicly expressed our willingness to renew bilateral talks with the Chinese in Warsaw or elsewhere. Ambassador Stoessel in Warsaw was authorized by the president to tell his Chinese colleague of the president's wish to discuss an improvement in relations. All these statements and positions, including liberalization of American travel and tourist purchases of Chinese products, were favorably received by the great majority of our newspapers and members of Congress.

Whereas the Chinese early in 1969 had castigated the Nixon Administration in the harshest terms, attacks moderated in the course of the year. Previously, Chinese representatives conveyed to a number of foreigners their awareness that US policy toward China was under review. However they also made it clear that the issue of Taiwan, including US military forces deployed there, created a major obstacle to any Sino–US rapprochement. We also received indirect official word from Beijing that China appreciated US restraint in not seeking to exploit the Sino-Soviet dispute and that the US obviously did not see a Sino-Soviet war as being in its interests.

There were misgivings expressed by some of our Soviet experts about President Nixon's interest in a *rapprochement* with China lest it sour our all-too-delicate relations with the USSR. I recall my long conversation with Llewellyn Thompson, then senior adviser on Soviet affairs in the State Department. He raised his concerns on this subject.

I responded that I had discussed the issue at length with the president on our flight from Midway to Hawaii in June 1969. The president seemed determined to handle **any** US-Chinese rapprochement in a way which would not impair US-Soviet relations. Moreover, he had told a group of our ambassadors on July 30, 1969 in Bangkok: "As far as the Sino-Soviet controversy is concerned, we must not line up with either Moscow or Beijing. China's billion people and nuclear potential offer an unpleasant prospect, but so does Soviet adventurism in Asia." (quoted from Green travel diary.) Later Nixon tilted more toward China.

In late 1969 the US announced that it would automatically validate passports for travel to the PRC for members of Congress, journalists, teachers, scholars, medical doctors and Red Cross representatives. Foreign subsidiaries of American companies would be permitted to sell China non-strategic items of foreign manufacture, while US companies were permitted to buy or sell Chinese goods within or between foreign countries but not to import Chinese goods to the US. US tourist purchases of Chinese goods were allowed without limit.

Our bureau was encouraged by the interest shown by the president in all these moves to ease restrictions on US-Chinese trade and travel, although we were pressing for a complete lifting of all travel restrictions on Americans desiring to visit China, and on all restrictions on Chinese *bona fide* visitors to the US. These steps were finally approved by the White House in March and April of 1971.

In his Foreign Policy Message to Congress in February 1970, Mr. Nixon declared that the US aim was to establish a "more normal and constructive relationship with Communist China." He asserted that the US had "historic ties of friendship with the Chinese people, and many of our basic interests are not in conflict."

Early in 1970 there were encouraging developments in the ambassadorial-level talks that had been going on for many years in Prague and then in Warsaw. The Chinese were surprisingly responsive to a proposal by Ambassador Stoessel (on White House approved instructions from the Department) for an exchange of high-level emissaries to discuss ways to reduce tensions between China and the US.

The Department hesitated to move ahead without a clear sign from Beijing that it would react constructively on the basic issues at stake. As I said in a note to Mr. Kissinger, to do so without any such clarification would risk setting back the clock. State also suspected that Beijing's approval might be more tactical than substantive, perhaps using the presence of a US delegation in China as a mere make-weight in their border talks with Moscow. We also had to consider how such talks would impact on Japan and other allies.

In his memoirs (*White House Years*, page 691), Mr. Kissinger criticizes State's reservations on this issue, yet it would seem that his own advance secret mission to China in 1971 was essential for establishing the basis for President Nixon's successful trip to Beijing in February 1972.

Beijing's policy-makers must have given a lot of thought to its fundamental differences with Hanoi that assumed new dimensions following the deposing of Prince Sihanouk by General Lon Nol in mid-March 1970, and Sihanouk's subsequent flight to Beijing via Moscow.

This event brought out even more clearly how the motives of Beijing and Hanoi differed, though appearances were kept to the contrary. Obviously Beijing would not take measures in regard to Hanoi which might strengthen

Moscow's standing there, if it could avoid them (although events were leading in this direction).

The subsequent (April 30, 1970) US–South Vietnamese incursion into Cambodia may have affected our prospects for improvement in US–China relations. In any case the presidential decision to involve US ground forces in this Cambodian incursion required the president to over-ride State Department objections, which probably left him determined to play his diplomatic cards on sensitive issues even closer to his chest (as he was to do in carrying out his trip to China almost two years later).

At our Chiefs of Mission meeting in Tokyo in July 1970, we concluded that:

1) Beijing is on the defensive, acutely worried about the Soviet military buildup in Siberia and Moscow's growing influence with Hanoi.

(2) It is worried that the US will be pulling back militarily from the Western Pacific, and is apprehensive about future Japanese capabilities and interests.

(3) It is determined to heal the scars of the Cultural Revolution, and rebuild the Party and the economy. The latter will entail a trade relationship with the US which advances China's development.

These and other conclusions of the Conference, which was attended by Secretary Rogers, were forwarded to President Nixon in a memorandum I drafted which concluded:

"We have no reason to apologize for the past. The very protection we extended to the nations of Asia these last two decades has now permitted us to draw back somewhat and, indeed, to focus on the dangers of our over-involvement (as in Vietnam) and unwarranted tutelage. This is not a question of getting out of Asia, but of finding the right way and right degree of staying in Asia . . . . We accept the risks and yet the ultimate safety of involvement."

All the back channel soundings that the president and Kissinger were making to Beijing through third countries and various intermediaries in early 1971 were carried out under the strictest security precautions, leaving us in the State Department completely in the dark, except for the Secretary of State who was kept partially informed.

On the other hand, we recognized that the massive build up of Soviet military power in Siberia, hard along the northern frontier of China, was profoundly disturbing to the Chinese leadership. This would entail a re-evaluation of China's policy towards the great powers.

The first overt indications of a new Chinese policy towards the United States took a curious form. During an international ping-pong tournament in Japan in April 1971, the Chinese team invited the American team to visit China, an invitation the US accepted and reciprocated. Shortly thereafter, the White House authorized the State and Commerce Departments to liberalize foreign assets control regulations affecting US trade with China. Win Brown and Bob Barnett spent many days with their Commerce colleagues working out necessary changes in the Federal Register.

US policy towards China, and the Chinese representation issue in the UN, were major topics for discussion at our Chiefs of Mission meeting which I chaired in Baguio, the Philippines, May 17-20, 1971.

Walter McConaughy, our ambassador to the Republic of China on Taiwan, reluctantly concluded that a change of US tactics would be required if there were to be any real chance of preventing the ouster or walk-out of Taibei representatives at the UNGA session in October. Eight more countries had recognized Beijing during the previous few months, and even Taibei itself realized that perhaps a dual representation formula (seating both Chinas in the UN) was its only chance for survival in the UN. However it remained adamant, according to McConaughy, that Taibei represent China in the UN Security Council — a solution Beijing would almost certainly reject.

Our Consulate General in Hong Kong, represented by Consul General David Osborn, made what turned out to be a remarkably prophetic analysis of the terms under which a Washington-Beijing rapprochement could be achieved **without** the US abandoning its commitments to Taiwan:

1)"Regarding the status of Taiwan, we should say that we do not disagree with claims of both parties that Taiwan is a province of China. We are deluding ourselves if we believe we can have good relations with the Peoples' Republic without such a declaration.

2)"No need to remove our military forces from Taiwan completely to have better relations with the mainland. We must, however, start moving in that direction.

3)"We should de-emphasize verbally our bilateral security treaty with the GRC (Taibei), while keeping that treaty in force.

4)"We should continue to favor a peaceful resolution of GRC-PRC problems through direct talks, but we should low-key this in our public output. Usually it is better for us to say nothing and let the countries directly concerned work out their own problems."

Osborn and I agreed that Beijing was now moving in a more pragmatic direction, making it probable that it would accept a US position embodying the above four points.

Meanwhile, as earlier stated, unbeknownst to any of us in the State Department (except Secretary Rogers), Henry Kissinger and a few key White House colleagues were involved in highly secret preparations for Kissinger's trip to China in June 1971.

The president had a passion for secrecy based in part on his distrust of the bureaucracy. Never was secrecy more strictly pursued than it was over preparing for the Kissinger trip, and with considerable justification. Had word leaked out, it might have raised all kinds of criticisms from the right wing of the Republican party, not to mention deep concern in Taiwan, Japan and other countries affected.

So I am not faulting Nixon and Kissinger for some secrecy in diplomacy, but not informing people who are expected to be informed can give rise to some real dangers. Let me cite a specific example. I recall meeting one morning in early July 1971 with several key members of my staff, one of whom mentioned that it had just been announced over the radio that Kissinger, who was in Pakistan on a round-the-world trip, had contracted a case of intestinal flu, and was therefore planning to take several days rest by motoring up from Islamabad to the Pakistan mountain resort area of Murree.

I commented to my staff that this was ridiculous — that no one with that affliction would take off on a long bumpy motor trip. I then observed that Henry was probably off on a secret trip to China.

As soon as I said those words, it occurred to me that my impromptu speculation, if true, would immediately spread to the newspapers, and I would be responsible for the worst leak of the Nixon administration. So I quickly excused myself from my meeting, dashed up to Secretary Rogers' office, and told him what had happened. The Secretary paled visibly, for I had uncovered the truth. On his instructions, I rushed back to my office and swore all present to utter secrecy about my speculation. They kept the secret.

Such are the dangers of not telling officials of events occurring in their area of responsibility.

Right after the president amazed the world with his widely televised revelations in the summer of 1971 about Henry's trip to Beijing and plans for the president to visit China the following February, I received a phone call from Secretary Rogers who was with Nixon in San Clemente. He asked what I thought of the announcement. I said it was great, but that we were going to have problems with the Japanese.

Secretary Rogers seemed surprised, pointing out that we had given Prime Minister Sato several hours advance notice of the president's announcement (as indeed we had to other allies). I said that the announcement nevertheless left Prime Minister Sato in a most embarrassing political position. For years we had been urging restraint on other countries about opening relations with Beijing; and the Japanese, largely out of deference to us, had continued to vote in the UN against seating Beijing's representatives in China's UN seat. And now we had secretly reached Beijing before Japan, exposing the Japanese government to the first of what were to be several "Nixon Shockus" that rocked US–Japanese relations.

Anyway, I told Secretary Rogers that Dick Ericson (Director of Japanese Affairs) and I would work immediately on a draft message from Nixon to Sato explaining the reasons for tight security and apologizing for any embarrassments this might have caused our most important Asian ally. Our draft message, telexed to San Clemente, was approved by the president, but I doubt it did much to allay Sato's concerns.

In his memoirs published in 1984, Under Secretary U. Alexis Johnson, a former US Ambassador to Japan and close friend of Sato, revealed that he had been alerted by Nixon to fly out to Tokyo to give Sato advance notice and thus demonstrate special consideration for Japan. But for some reason the White House cancelled the Johnson trip.

The president's announcement was an even greater shock to President Chiang and his government, but there wasn't much we could do to reduce it. Indeed, the president's impending trip to China had the effect of completely undermining the position our government had taken year after year in marshalling international support for Taiwan retaining China's seat in the UN.

Not that I found this to be any great loss, because the eventual seating of the PRC was inevitable. Nevertheless we in the State Department were under orders from Nixon in 1971, even after the president's China trip was announced, to do what we could to preserve the GRC's position in the UN. It took a lot of our time and effort — and eventually we lost.

During the autumn of 1971, John Service, who in the 1940's was the most able of all the State Department China language officers and who was later hounded out of the service by McCarthyism, made a trip to China with his wife Caroline as personal guests of Premier Zhou Enlai. I, as Jack's close friend from the days back in 1946–47 when we had served together in New Zealand, visited the Services on their return to Berkeley, California. Jack gave me a detailed account of his China trip as we walked over the nearby hills.

Jack met with the top leaders whom he had known from the World War II days when they were together in the Yenan Caves. He found the Cultural Revolution rapidly subsiding. It was clear that Zhou Enlai, in particular, was preparing the way for serious productive talks with Nixon. The key issue would be Taiwan. Zhou recognized that the US could not switch its policy overnight and that some evolution over time would be required. From Beijing's viewpoint, it was absolutely essential that the US not promote or encourage any Taiwan independence movement. If the US looked for a successful outcome of President Nixon's trip, it must accept Taiwan as an integral part of China. Of less immediate consequence was the removal of US forces from Taiwan.

Especially interesting was his account of the notable improvements that had taken place in the lives of most Chinese people over the last two decades. Jack reported Zhou's surprise over the PRC victory (October 25, 1971) on the UN seating issue. The Chinese clearly hadn't anticipated this favorable result. During his conversation with Zhou Enlai on October 27, 1971, there were constant staff interruptions with regard to developments in New York and hasty arrangements being made for China's participation in the UN. I reported Jack's views to the White House, State and CIA.

The Service visit coincided by chance with another Henry Kissinger trip to China, as our dialogue with Beijing began to expand. To follow these events we turn to the perspective of John Holdridge, who as a White House staff member had a unique awareness of presidential initiatives on China.

PART III

THE PATH TO PEACE

by John H. Holdridge

CHAPTER 8

SINO–US CONTACTS DURING THE FREEZE

After the Korean War, I was able to follow US-China relations closely from assignments in the China Desk of the State Department and Hong Kong, our main China-watching field post. Despite the continuing tone of hostility, the two countries maintained fairly regular contacts, at first in a multilateral setting.

The Panmunjom talks which resulted in the Korean truce were followed by the talks in Geneva to end the fighting between the Viet Minh and the French in Indochina. The US was represented at the Geneva talks by US Secretary of State John Foster Dulles, and China by Premier Zhou Enlai.

Edwin M. Martin, a member of the US delegation, told me that a Chinese counterpart of his had hinted that after the Korean truce was reached a "stage" in Sino-US relations had been passed and that a "new stage" might be possible. Both during and after the Geneva talks, consular representatives of the two sides met from time to time in Geneva to discuss continuing detention of each other's nationals.

The next dialogue followed the Non-Aligned Conference in Bandung, Indonesia in 1955 when Zhou Enlai used a press conference to propose high-level US-Chinese talks to reduce tensions, notably those arising from the Taiwan issue. Secretary Dulles' initial reaction was to say "no," but after thinking the matter over he suggested that the consular-level contacts at Geneva be raised to the ambassadorial level. The first in a long series of talks began in August between U. Alexis Johnson our ambassador in Prague and Wang Bingnan, China's ambassador in Warsaw.

The US wanted above all release of its citizens being held in China, while the Chinese pressed for a broad review of US-Chinese differences, including withdrawal of US forces from the Taiwan Strait. An "Agreed Announcement" was arrived at on September 10, 1955 calling for "appropriate" measures to be taken by each side to allow citizens of the other to "expeditiously exercise their right to return;" and "other practical matters at issue."

Early in the talks the Chinese freed 41 of the Americans detained in China after the US permitted all Chinese students and teachers in the US to return to China if they wished to do so. Despite the Agreed Announcement the Chinese kept many Americans who had been convicted of violating Chinese laws under detention pending expiration of their sentences, thus generating US resentment over what was taken to be Chinese bad faith.

On the Taiwan issue, the US proposed that neither side be required to renounce its views but agree to pursue its policies peacefully. Each side would retain the right to defend itself, but both countries would renounce the use of force, both generally and specifically in the Taiwan area.

Wang's counter-draft referred to the obligations of member states of the UN to settle international disputes peacefully and stated, "The PRC and the US declared that they should settle disputes between the two countries without resorting to the threat or use of force," and called for a meeting of foreign ministers to address the matter of "relaxing and eliminating the tension in the Taiwan area." Wang's approach would have had the effect of separating the Taiwan issue from the ambassadorial-level talks and from the list of matters which could be settled peacefully. In addition, a bilateral meeting between Dulles and Zhou Enlai would be a step toward US recognition of China. (The Geneva talks of 1954 on Vietnam were multilateral.) Accordingly, the US rejected the formulation presented by Wang and both sides adhered to their positions. The US then made release of Americans still detained in China a precondition for further progress on other issues.

Secretary Dulles kept a careful eye on the Geneva talks, and in fact made his own input into the discussions. In late 1956, when I was temporarily detailed to the talks as a rapporteur, I heard Ambassador Johnson say that when Wang's formulation on settling the dispute in the Taiwan Strait reached Washington and a reply was being drafted, Dulles personally inserted the phrase "including the dispute in the Taiwan Strait" after Wang's wording on settling disputes between the two countries peacefully. Dulles, an international lawyer by profession, clearly wanted to leave no ambiguities in the US response but Wang refused to accept the reformulation.

While this exchange was going on Zhou Enlai introduced another element: mutual travel of journalists from each country to the other. To do so, he removed a Chinese ban on travel to China by US newsmen, and sent invitations to fifteen US news-gathering organizations to send representatives for a one month tour. Not unexpectedly, Secretary Dulles refused, but a year later, when the pressure of adverse criticism from organizations on Zhou's list and from the press in general mounted, he finally relented and permitted 24 US news organizations to send representatives to China. They could remain, he said, for a six-month trial period which could be extended if they were permitted to report freely. There was to be no reciprocity for Chinese journalists unless they were able on a case-by-case basis to meet US visa requirements. This proposal Wang rejected.

The talks were nearing an impasse, although they did continue sporadically until December 1957 when Johnson informed Wang that he would be leaving the talks to assume his new post in Bangkok. His replacement would be his deputy, Edwin Martin, who would be given the personal rank of Minister. Wang forthwith protested this move as an attempt to downgrade the talks and refused to set a date for the next meeting.

Seven months later Jacob Beam was named US Ambassador in Warsaw (where Wang was also accredited) and US delegate to the talks, thus meeting the last Chinese objection. The Chinese initially did not respond to this effort to reopen the talks. The delay may have been due to an impending attack on Quemoy and Matsu, which led to a near–confrontational situation with the US in August and September 1958. Zhou Enlai then sought to cool the crisis by proposing to resume the talks and to use them "for the defense of peace." In the broadcast in which Zhou made this proposal, he also accused Taibei of attempting to use the offshore islands as bases from which to attack the China mainland.

The US accepted Zhou's proposal. In the give-and-take with Wang, Beam noted that while the US would not allow the offshore islands to change hands, it would "respond to a Communist ceasefire by persuading the Nationalists to forego the use of Quemoy and Matsu as bases for attacks against the mainland." In taking this position, he was responding to an estimate of US public opinion to the effect that, while the territorial integrity of Taiwan remained fully supported, this same public opinion would not condone the use of Quemoy and Matsu as sites from which to attack the China mainland.

The position taken by Beam was formalized in a joint communique signed by Dulles and Chiang Kai-shek in Taibei on October 23, 1958. Dulles accepted the defense of Quemoy, Matsu, and the Pescadores (a small island chain in the mid–Taiwan Strait region) as being closely related to the defense of Taiwan, while the ROC, under considerable prodding, declared that "the principal means of successfully achieving its mission ["the restoration of freedom to its people on the mainland"] is by the implementation of Dr. Sun Yat-sen's Three People's Principles and not the use of force." (Despite this commitment it did try later a landing on the island of Hainan, which was unsuccessful.) Marshall Green had an influential role in formulating this position and in gaining acceptance of it by Chiang.

With the "Taiwan Strait crisis" under control, the ambassadorial talks turned into a rather sterile exchange, until some twelve years later. Meanwhile, to downplay the fact that the PRC had backed down, China kept up a strange alternate-day artillery bombardment of Quemoy, using mainly propaganda shells, with the ROC forces on the islands replying in kind.

Bill Bundy later commented to me that there was, nevertheless, one important gain from this stage of the talks: the US was able to assure the Chinese that it bore no hostility toward China. Later, once the US involvement in Vietnam had begun, the US explained it was not attempting to destroy the Hanoi regime. These assurances may have had a bearing on future Chinese assessments of the US "threat" once the winds of change began to blow.

CHAPTER 9

THE GLACIER STARTS MELTING

After many years of glacial relations between the US and China, 1968 brought something of a thaw. The USSR had only itself to blame for this change, through its promulgation of the "Brezhnev Doctrine," which arrogated to the Soviet Union as the so-called "vanguard party" within the bloc of Communist states the right to define the proper "road to socialism" - and to take action against deviations.

Doctrine became reality when the Soviets occupied Prague on August 21, 1968, to end the Czech deviationism begun by Dubcek. The Chinese got the message quite rapidly: if the USSR was capable of using force against one "fraternal socialist state" for taking what the USSR saw as a wrong road, the Chinese, who were following an even more deviant road, were also vulnerable. In fact the Chinese for years had been carrying on an ideological polemic with the Soviets over the means of achieving the victory of socialism. They rejected peaceful economic competition, as espoused by Moscow, in favor of "revolutionary struggle," not flinching at bloodshed.

After the Prague episode heated discussions must have taken place within the Chinese leadership on how to react, concluding that the enemies arrayed against China should be reduced by one, i.e. the US. As early as September the Chinese replied favorably and promptly to a US proposal to restart the Warsaw talks. By November agreement to resume them was reached, but they did not take place as scheduled.

Editorials in *People's Daily, Red Flag,* and other CCP journals cast aspersions on "peaceful coexistence," thus casting a shadow over the talks. Then the Chinese Chargé in The Hague sought asylum in the US Embassy. When the

Chinese demanded his return and were refused, the Chinese called off the scheduled talks.

My own speculation is that the elements in Chinese politics who later became known as the '"Gang of Four:" Mao Zedong's wife Jiang Qing, Shanghai Mayor Zhang Qunqiao, Wang Hungwen, who later was named as Mao's putative successor, and Minister of Culture Yao Wenyuan, were involved in initiating the counter-current. Others in State shared this judgment with me. (At this time I was Office Director of the Office of Research and Analysis for East Asia and the Pacific, or INR/REA.)

In the meantime, Soviet transgressions against China became publicly known. Zhou Enlai charged that over the years the Soviets had violated Chinese borders more than 2000 times by aircraft overflights, by incursions of military personnel, and by Soviet shipping on the Amur and Ussuri rivers sailing through Chinese waters. Zhou and CCP party publications also declared that hundreds of thousands of square miles of Chinese territory had been occupied during the time of the Czars via unequal treaties.

To make the point that China possessed military teeth capable of inflicting damage on the USSR, an Albanian military delegation was taken to Shuangchengzu, the Chinese missile test-bed and launching site. China had tested its first nuclear device in 1964, and now showed that it had a nuclear missile launch capability.

Not long afterwards Soviet and Chinese troops fought over control of a small island in the Ussuri River. Chinese border guards first drove Soviet troops off the island, and then were driven off themselves as the result of a massive Soviet artillery bombardment. The long-simmering ideological dispute between the USSR and China thus turned into a nationalistic dispute.

At least one effort was made to ease the military tensions between the two countries. In September, 1969, when Soviet President Kosygin made a refueling stop at Beijing airport on his return to Moscow from attending Ho Chi Minh's funeral in Hanoi (Ho had died on September 3), Zhou Enlai met him at the airport. In the VIP lounge the two went over steps which could be taken to address the issues which had arisen between the USSR and China. From Chinese sources I later heard that Kosygin had agreed with Zhou on a number of sore points. These agreements included setting up a commission to resolve the issue of the riverine boundary, pulling back both sides' troops 20 kilometers from the border, and the holding of talks to discuss the actual location of Sino-Soviet borders. But, according to these same sources, all of what Kosygin had agreed to was repudiated by the Soviets once he was back in Moscow. The Chinese were deeply offended by this repudiation.

Following Kosygin's return to Moscow, a rapid and extremely heavy Soviet military build-up took place along the Sino-Soviet and Sino-Mongolian People's Republic borders, to which the Chinese were obliged to respond to the best of their abilities. A Soviet "Front" headquarters was set up in this region, and military tensions remained high, along with political tensions. As far as the US was concerned, there was little that could be done at the time to advance the cause of improved Sino-US relations. But as we have shown, a start had been made by the Department of State, despite the subsequent efforts by the new Nixon Administration to depict State as lacking imagination and drive in its approach to China policy.

Nixon's Initiatives

Marshall Green's talks with Richard Nixon, described in an earlier chapter, appeared to bear fruit from the beginning of Nixon's tenure as president. Nixon's rationale, which I often heard him express to visiting VIPs after I joined the National Security Council (NSC) staff in mid-1969, was "It's far better to talk to the Chinese than to fight them," given China's huge population (then over 600 million people), key geographic location, and important world-wide strategic, economic, and political influence.

Soon after his inauguration Nixon ordered a policy study of Sino-US relations to assess a change in US policy, via a process involving "NSSMs" (National Security Study Memos) and "NSDMs" (National Security Decision Memos). The format and terms of reference for these were laid out by the NSC, but farmed out to key US Government agencies for drafting. The whole process was overseen by a Senior Interdepartmental Group (SIG), chaired by a senior officer of the Department of State, who would see that the various drafts were pulled together for decision by the president. Once the president had signed off, the NSDM was issued to the entire Government by the NSC.

About the time that the draft on China (NSSM 14) was completed, I was assigned to the NSC from the State Department as Senior Staff Member for East Asia, and had a chance to observe the NSSM's progress from both ends. Earlier in the SIG group I had recommended several unilateral moves which the US might take to improve Sino-US relations: relaxation of the embargo on export of certain non-strategic US goods to China, and elimination of the hardly-enforceable "certificate of origin" requirement on importation of goods of a Chinese nature into the US to assure that they didn't come from China. The SIG was chaired by Winthrop

Brown, senior Deputy Assistant Secretary. Its recommendations were accepted by the Administration and put into
effect between July and December. More unilateral moves
toward China followed, notably cessation of US patrols in
the Taiwan Strait and further relaxations on trade and travel
of Americans to China.

The president then embarked on a world tour in July
1969 (to Guam, Manila, Jakarta, Bangkok, Saigon, Lahore,
and Bucharest before returning to the US) and I was in the
party. The first stop was on Johnson Island for splash-down
of the first US moon landing mission, then to Guam. While
on the ensuing presidential flight between Jakarta and
Bangkok, Dr. Kissinger asked me to draft a message to the
Chinese proposing that China and the US get together to
explore the possibility of improving relations. I responded
with a draft along the lines that while we had encountered
many differences during the last two decades, we should now
look to the future rather than to the past to see where
differences could be reconciled.

Kissinger took my draft with a characteristic grunt (one
with which I became familiar in the coming years) and
walked with it in the direction of the president's quarters.
Also characteristically, I never had any feedback. I cannot
but believe, however, that something at least similar to what
I had drafted was actually sent to the Chinese, either from
Lahore through the Pakistanis, who had very good relations
with China, or from Bucharest where Ceausescu maintained
good ties with Beijing.

The method used aboard Air Force One by the president
and Dr. Kissinger to approach the Chinese provided a
foretaste of how foreign policy was to be managed in the
future, including (but not limited to) Sino-US relations. The
policy center was to be in the White House and not in State,
which was to be kept out of all substantive decisions and

limited to a supporting role in filling out details once a main course of action had been decided. As far as China was concerned, State had very little input. The president's attitude toward State was made plain in November, 1969, when in a meeting with the entire NSC senior staff in the Cabinet Room, he told us that foreign policy was our business and would be handled directly by the White House. The occasion was the issuance of the first of several annual reports to the Congress on foreign policy, which had been drafted entirely by the NSC without any input, or even clearance, from State.

President Nixon's disdainful attitude toward State was probably due in part to the rather casual attitude displayed toward him by many Foreign Service posts during a world-wide tour he had made as a private citizen after his term as vice president. (Marshall Green gives below an additional theory on this point.) Nevertheless, he retained confidence in some Foreign Service officers, including Marshall Green and U. Alexis Johnson. Perhaps he was unaware that about 50 percent of the NSC senior staffers he was addressing were FSOs, but in any event, his lack of confidence in State made my own life very difficult. Over the next four years, my opposite number in State was primarily Marshall Green (who may have owed his appointment as Assistant Secretary for East Asia and the Pacific to the president's recollection of his 1967 talk with Marshall in Jakarta). I had constant need to cross-reference matters with him.

Regardless of what message was sent to China during the president's July, 1969 world tour, and by what means, there was no quick response from China. It can be speculated that the Chinese were still sorting out the signals from the US. At any rate, the US Ambassador to Warsaw, Walter Stoessel (who was now the US representative on the Warsaw talks), in October was directed to propose once again a resumption of the talks. I sat in on the Kissinger-Stoessel meeting in the White House.

Much to Kissinger's annoyance, finding the appropriate moment took some time. He blamed State for the delay. I knew Walt Stoessel too well to believe that there was any deliberate holding back, and eventually the contact was made on December 3 when Walt stopped Charge Lei Yang and his interpreter as they all were leaving (incongruously) a Yugoslav fashion show. Walt passed on his message and Lei Yang said he would inform his government.

The response was swift. Within a matter of days Lei Yang appeared at the American Embassy in Warsaw in his "Red Flag" limousine flying China's five-star flag, to convey the Chinese acceptance. Walt reciprocated shortly afterward by calling on Lei Yang in his Cadillac flying the Stars and Stripes. Beijing and Washington announced simultaneously that the talks would resume in Warsaw on January 20, 1970. The US spokesman in Washington, in announcing the event, was careful to refer to China for the first time by the US as the "People's Republic of China." The stage was now set for a better relationship.

CHAPTER 10

THROUGH CHINA'S BACK DOOR

When the Warsaw talks actually resumed, instructions for the opening meeting sent by State to Stoessel (and of course cleared by the White House) contained a dramatic new element: the suggestion that each side send high-level emissaries to the other's capital to discuss both differences and what could be done to reduce them and improve relations.

The suggestion for the exchange of high-level emissaries was generated entirely by State. Stoessel was told to express the "hope" that as tensions in the Taiwan region abated, US troop strength there could be reduced.

The officers most immediately identified with the drafting of these instructions were Assistant Secretary Green, his deputy Winthrop Brown, and Paul Kreisberg, Office Director of "Asian Communist Areas" (ACA), all Foreign Service career officers.

At the January 20 meeting, after Walt Stoessel's words had sunk in, Lei Yang responded, as expected, that he would inform his government about the US proposal. He then went on to say:

"We are willing to consider and discuss whatever ideas and suggestions the US Government might put forward in accordance with the five principles of peaceful coexistence, therefore really helping to reduce tensions between China and the US and fundamentally improve relations between China and the US. These talks may be conducted at the ambassadorial level, or may be conducted at a higher level or through other channels acceptable to both sides." (See Seymour Hersh, *The Price of Power*, p. 361.)

Lei's response indicated that Beijing must have been carefully monitoring the exchange and evidently had an inkling in advance of what the US might propose.

Before the next meeting, on February 20, new complications on the US side arose. I was the first on the NSC staff to see State's new draft instructions, and was more than a little surprised to see that there was no follow-up on the exchange of high-level emissaries. Such an omission would have almost certainly created negative reactions in Beijing, a point which I called to Dr. Kissinger's attention.

In *The White House Years*, Kissinger suggests various reasons why State got cold feet, which to him revolved about the presumed adverse effects on US allies in the EA region, especially Taiwan, as well as on neutrals and the USSR, without any tangible gain. In any event, State was duly directed to carry on with the high-level exchange idea. It was also to make conciliatory statements vis-a-vis China which would separate it as an adversary in US policy-making. Stoessel was instructed to say at the February 20 meeting that, "It is my Government's **intention** (no longer a 'hope') to reduce those facilities which we have in the Taiwan area as tensions in the area diminish."

The Chinese response was to accept the US proposal to send a high-level US emissary be sent to Beijing for talks there.

Major complications then set in, involving a debate between the White House and State on the desirability of actually sending a high-level US emissary to Beijing. There was also no agreement on the timing of the next Warsaw meeting. As State perceived the issue, the Chinese would probably exploit the signs of US flexibility to gain influence in East Asia at US expense, particularly regarding North Vietnam, Japan, and the USSR. Also, a hostile reaction could be expected from the Congress. Accordingly, State wanted to hold back the momentum of the emissary issue by first enquiring into the conditions under which the emissary would be received. On the White House side, it was perceived that any delay would be likely to sink the new approach to China without a trace.

When the tortured history of US-China tensions is taken into account, as well as the long-standing US recognition of Taiwan as the sole representative of "China," State's reservations were understandable. What State did not know, and what would have helped considerably to clear the air, was the record of White House efforts to open communications with the Chinese, including "back-channel" messages through CIA stations in Romania or Pakistan. This was a system with only a very few people involved and no copies to State or indeed any US Government agency.

Further drawing the US into the problems surrounding the Warsaw talks was the North Vietnamese reaction to the anti-Sihanouk coup in Cambodia. For a few days after the coup, the North Vietnamese and Viet Cong took no action. Then their forces east of the Mekong began to attack Cambodian army units between the South Vietnamese border and Phnom Penh to maintain unimpeded access to the "sanctuary" provided by this territory for operations against South Vietnam. As a result, by April 18, the ill-led and ill-equipped Cambodians had retreated to a line along the Bassac River, only five kilometers from Phnom Penh.

With this development a full-scale military collapse by the Cambodians seemed possible, especially in the "sanctuary" areas, with incalculable effects on the policy of "Vietnamization" which the US was following in Vietnam, i.e. turning the fighting over to the South Vietnamese as they were armed and trained and as US troops withdrew. The full National Security Council met on April 22 to consider the consequences of a Communist victory in Cambodia, and initiated a series of steps designed to block a Communist victory. One of these was a US and South Vietnamese attack across the Cambodian border against the Communist sanctuaries and headquarters area beginning on May 1 and lasting until June 30. Regardless of the merits of this operation (which the State Department was over-ruled in opposing) it had the side-effect of halting the US-PRC talks in Warsaw in their tracks.

Regarding the Warsaw talks, the White House and State finally had agreed after considerable argumentation to hold the next meeting on April 30, or on any subsequent date convenient to the Chinese. One issue in this wrangling was the scheduled visit April 22 to the US of Chiang Chingkuo, at that time Vice-Premier of the ROC. When the April 30 date was offered in Warsaw to the Chinese, they turned it down and suggested May 20, which the US accepted. However, after this date was set, harsh and increasingly vituperative criticism of the US operation in Cambodia emanated from the Beijing press. A statement by the New China News Agency (NCNA) on May 18, carried in a box on the front page of all major newspapers, declared that in view of the US "invasion" of Cambodia it would be "inappropriate" for the talks to continue. It was signed simply "Mao Zedong."

Thereafter, for the rest of 1970 there was no direct contact between the US and China. Dr. Kissinger moved to back-channel communications to try to keep the China contact going. Representatives of other countries were asked to act as postmen, both in their own nations and in Washington. A significant stage in this activity came when a large number of chiefs of state or heads of government came to the US in October, 1970, to participate in celebrations of the 25th anniversary of the founding of the United Nations. They were asked by President Nixon to attend a state dinner in the White House in honor of the event.

This dinner turned out to be quite a remarkable affair, since it brought together leaders from both East and West, hostile and non–hostile alike, to Washington. Emperor Haile Selassie of Ethiopia, the senior personage present, was guest of honor. An American aide was supplied for each dignitary during the reception in the East Room of the White House which preceded the dinner. I found myself escorting the Vice President of the ROC, Chen Cheng, and actually introducing him to Rumanian President Nicolae Ceausescu. During the dinner Nixon used Ceausescu's presence to offer a toast, which while alluding to the many common interests held by the people of the US and Romania and to the good relations which Romania had with the US, the USSR, and China, referred to the latter country as the "People's Republic of China." This was the first use by an American President of China's official name.

Earlier that day, during a meeting in the Oval Office with President Yahya Khan of Pakistan, who was known to be planning a visit to Beijing in November, President Nixon referred to a US rapprochement with China as essential. He asserted that the US would not join in a conspiracy against China, and offered to send a high-level secret envoy to Beijing. He named retired senior diplomat Robert Murphy, former Governor Thomas Dewey, and Dr. Kissinger, as possible choices. In another Oval Office meeting with Ceausescu, he took the same line, except that with the latter he emphasized his desire for good relations with both China and the Soviet Union. (Kissinger, *The White House Years.*)

To make his intentions even clearer, President Nixon said in an interview carried in an October 1970 issue of *Time* that he hoped before he died to be able to visit China, and that he looked upon China as a world power, if not today, then in 20 years; if he couldn't make the trip, he added, he wished that his children could. A bit later, when President Yahya

Khan returned from a five-day China visit which had lasted from November 10 to 15, Pakistani Ambassador Hilaly in Washington informed the White House that a "message" had been brought back by Yahya Khan from Zhou Enlai for the president. The message was on behalf of not only Zhou himself, but also Chairman Mao Zedong and Vice Chairman Lin Biao. It stated that China had always wanted to settle the Taiwan issue peacefully with the US and was willing to receive a special envoy in Beijing for this purpose. Zhou further acknowledged in this message that he had received numerous communications from the US, but this was the first (to quote Dr. Kissinger) to come "from a Head, through a Head, to a Head. . . . The United States knows that Pakistan is a great friend of China and therefore we attach importance to the message." Thus, China signified its willingness to accept a high-level envoy to Beijing, but also signalled an intention to focus the discussions on the Taiwan question.

Secret, Back-Door Flight to Beijing, July 1971

Dr. Kissinger called me to his office in the early spring of 1971 to tell me that we were back on track and that I should get busy with "the books:" loose-leaf binders with papers describing what we thought about the current Chinese situation, what his visit was intended to accomplish, and his opening statement.

There followed position papers designed to touch on every possible issue which the talks might embrace. Each paper included an outline of the specific issue under discussion, such as tensions on the Korean Peninsula, where China and the US shared a security stake, next a short outline of the anticipated Chinese position, and finally a step-by-step formulation of Dr. Kissinger's anticipated position entitled "your response." Such books were regularly prepared by Dr. Kissinger's staff for meetings with major opposite numbers. In this particular case, since security was so vital (Kissinger was particularly concerned about possible leaks from State) I did the preparations for my part of the exercise myself.

There were, though, two areas of concern outside my own sphere: Vietnam and the Soviet Union. In both of these Dr. Kissinger was deeply involved. The USSR section was prepared by him, possibly with the help of Winston Lord (I never asked) and the Vietnam portion at least in part, by William "Dick" Smyser, a Foreign Service officer with considerable Vietnam experience. Navy Captain, later Admiral, Jonathan Howe I believe prepared the strategic papers.

The rest were mine, which involved me in frequent planning sessions with Dr. Kissinger. Occasionally, instructions were relayed by Winston Lord. Kissinger would lay out a line to be followed in dealing with an issue, and I would fill in the blanks, drawing upon my experiences in East and Southeast Asia as derived from visits or assignments to the Philippines, Vietnam, Japan, Hong Kong, Taiwan, and Indonesia. Kissinger made few changes in my output and the work proceeded rapidly.

One aspect was particularly sensitive: the question of how to handle Taiwan, which was at the top of the Chinese agenda. I knew from Chinese propaganda that they were likely to accuse the US of trying to interfere in their relations with Taiwan and block the island's reunification with the mainland. Therefore, in Dr. Kissinger's opening statement I inserted language declaring that "the US was not seeking two Chinas, a one–China one–Taiwan solution, nor an independent Taiwan." Taiwan had been a key element in the Sino–US dispute for over two decades, had twice in the post-Korean War period almost brought the US into a shooting war (the evacuation of the Dachen Islands in 1955 and the defense of Quemoy and Matsu in 1958), and, to quote Pakistani Ambassador Hilaly's relayed message from Zhou Enlai, was the sole reason Zhou had agreed to high-level talks. In this light, the Taiwan issue had to be addressed as a priority matter so as to make it possible to discuss other problems of joint concern.

Fortunately, the Sino-Soviet ideological dispute was still continuing, the Soviet military threat against China had not abated, and it had become clear that the US had no hostile ambitions against China despite the Vietnam War.

The collective efforts of those working on the China trip received a stimulus with the publication in *Life* magazine (April 20, 1971 issue) of Edgar Snow's meeting with Chairman Mao in Beijing on December 10, 1970. Mao was quoted as telling Snow that he would be happy to talk to Nixon, whether as a tourist or as president, based on the fact that the US was getting out of Vietnam. These words from China's prime source were the first public endorsement by China on the prospects for a reduction in Sino-US tensions, and gave us in the NSC the belief that we were on the right track. President Nixon added to the good atmosphere by commenting on this article by observing that he would indeed like to visit China, along with his wife and daughters.

China Jumps Ahead with "Ping–Pong Diplomacy"

While we were hard at work preparing for the Kissinger China trip, Zhou Enlai took advantage of an international ping-pong match in Nagoya, Japan, in April, 1971, to put China out ahead in the publicity contest for credit in arranging improvement in Sino-US relations. After the match, the US team, which had competed with and lost to the Chinese, was invited by Zhou in the post-match friendly atmosphere, to visit China.

The White House approved the visit, which must have been inspired by Zhou Enlai himself. A reciprocal visit by the Chinese team later on was also approved by the White House. To drive home his advantage, Zhou emphasized in a speech during a reception in the Great Hall of the People for the US team that the visit opened up a new chapter in the history of the Chinese and American people. The world press, of course went wild. Obscured by all of this attention were continuing moves the US had been making to improve Sino-US relations such as broadening the removal of restrictions on travel to China by US citizens and on non-strategic trade between the US and China.

Behind the scenes, back channel messages between Beijing and Washington kept flowing, using Ambassador Farland in Islamabad as the conduit for the contact. Considerable haggling was necessary, for the Chinese continued to put the Taiwan issue first. The US, although accepting Taiwan as an agenda item, wished to add "other related issues." In this case, though, the earlier US and Chinese positions at the Geneva talks were reversed.

Eventually the Chinese accepted the added phrase, and Zhou Enlai and Dr. Kissinger were duly nominated as the two nations' high-level representatives. The meeting's date was set for July 9 in Beijing, even though this was not the best time for the Chinese, who were expecting North Korea's Kim Il Sung to be there at the same time.

Off Into the Unknown

I have noted that Dr. Kissinger was extremely careful about the security for the Beijing trip, and the whole venture was cloaked in extraordinary secrecy. For this reason, the Beijing visit was inserted into a tour of Vietnam, Thailand, India, and Pakistan, on the grounds that a visit to the Asian subcontinent by Dr. Kissinger was in order. Some commentators later maintained that the Japanese, at least, should have been informed in advance, but the NSC reasoning was that any word to Japanese Prime Minister Sato would have of necessity been used by him to protect his political flanks, and hence leaked. Public disclosure of the mission, according to Dr. Kissinger, would have caused us to negotiate China policy not with the Chinese, but with *The New York Times* and *The Washington Post*.

Travel as far as Pakistan, and after the China side-trip, back to the US was by US Government aircraft in order to provide secure communications. The only aircraft then available — Congressional travel having preempted all the others — was a KC-135 (a converted tanker) assigned to the Commanding General of the Air Force's Tactical Air Command. Except for Dr. Kissinger, who occupied a large, private cabin in the rear of the aircraft which had its own "head," there were few amenities. Seats and tables were close together, almost like rowing benches on an ancient galley. All our gear, including the precious books, was packed into this limited space.

In theory, our itinerary called for us to remain in Pakistan for 48 hours, the same amount of time spent in India so as to balance off these two hardly-friendly countries. The actual plan, though, called for Dr. Kissinger to start complaining about a stomach upset after arriving in Pakistan, giving President Yahya Khan an excuse to offer his rest house in Murree, a traditional hill station outside Islamabad, as a place in which to recover. An appropriate motorcade was even provided to travel to Murree, allegedly with Dr. Kissinger aboard, while the China party would slip away to make the trip to Beijing aboard a specially-configured Pakistan International Airlines Boeing 707.

At a dinner given before our departure by Yahya Khan on July 8, he informed Dr. Kissinger and me that Zhou Enlai had sent a group to escort us and reassure us about the welcome we would receive in Beijing. Sure enough, after our party (now limited to Dr. Kissinger, myself, Winston Lord, Dick Smyser, and two Secret Service agents) had left Yahya Khan's guest house about 3:30 a.m. and proceeded in civilian cars provided for cover to the military side of the Rawalpindi airport, four Chinese met us at the top of the ramp: Zhang Wenjin, a distinguished gentleman who had a long history of working closely with Zhou Enlai, Wang Hairong, Mao Zedong's grandniece, Tang Wensheng, known as Nancy Tang, an interpreter, and Tang Longbin, an official of the Chinese Foreign Ministry's Protocol Department. The aircraft, the engines of which had already started, took off without further delay.

The trip to Beijing was across some of the most spectacular mountain territory in the world, the Hindu Kush, and also across the most desolate, the Takla Makan, across which Silk Route caravans had wended their way. Upon reaching Beijing, we did not land at Beijing's international airport but at a special military airport south of the city where, as I later learned, China built its guided missiles. When we landed about mid-morning, Zhang Wenjin informed us that we were being met by Ye Jianying, a Marshal of the People's Liberation Army while rank designations still existed; Huang Hua, newly-appointed Ambassador to Canada; and Protocol Director Han Xu. Accompanying them as interpreter was Ji

Qaozhu, who had been trained at Tufts and Harvard. All of these figured prominently in the Sino-US relationship in the days and years to come.

We had hardly left the aircraft when an issue was raised with me by Huang Hua which evidently was much on the Chinese minds: the fact that US Secretary of State Dulles had refused to shake Premier Zhou Enlai's hand in Geneva back in 1954. I was surprised that Huang had raised this 17-year old issue with me, and calculated that despite all our exchanges in arranging the meeting in Beijing, the Chinese were still worried about another Dulles-type snub when Dr. Kissinger met with Zhou Enlai in a meeting to take place after our lunch. I immediately assured Huang Hua that we hadn't come all this distance in such a surreptitious way just to repeat the errors of the past, and that Zhou Enlai need have no fears about a handshake.

The destination of our motorcade was the Diao Yu Tai ("Fishing Pavilion"), which was the Chinese Government guest-house complex Northwest of Beijing and just outside the former city wall. By means of peeks taken through the car curtain next to me I saw enough of Beijing to remind me of a ghost city. Very few cars were on the streets, including on Chang An Jie, Beijing's main avenue, which runs in front of the Tien An Men, the Forbidden City's main gate. Likewise, there were very few pedestrians, and the people I did see looked like they were suffering some degree of combat fatigue as a result of the Cultural Revolution. Their faces were impassive, and their movements slow.

After our lunch Zhou Enlai arrived and his extended hand was promptly shaken by Dr. Kissinger, The entryway to our residence was then illuminated by a dazzling display of flash bulbs and high-intensity electric lights, as a whole host of Chinese newsmen and official photographers recorded this moment for posterity.

Henry Kissinger and Zhou Enlai greet each other on the first secret visit to China in 1971, redeeming the Dulles rebuff of Zhou's offered hand.

The negotiating parties at the first secret encounter, with Holdridge at the left of Zhou Enlai.

We next moved to a small conference room, where Zhou indicated that it was always the Chinese custom to let the guests speak first. Dr. Kissinger began by indulging in rather lengthy pleasantries while I waited impatiently for him to get to the point about Taiwan. He finally said what I had written for him on no two Chinas, no one China one Taiwan, no independent Taiwan. Zhou's response was immediate: "Good," he said, "these talks may now proceed." I am convinced that without this statement, any further discussions would have gotten nowhere if they continued at all.

In *The White House Years*, Kissinger noted that "Taiwan was mentioned only briefly during the first session," which was true, but which failed to observe that the Taiwan issue had been dealt with to the Chinese satisfaction from the very beginning, even if the problems over Taiwan had not been entirely eliminated.

Zhou and Dr. Kissinger then proceeded on that day and the next to embark on a wide-ranging review of world problems, which they both appeared to enjoy. From the very first meeting, Zhou did not speak from a book such as ours, but only from notes on a piece of paper. Not to be outdone, Dr. Kissinger (who surely was thoroughly familiar with the issues) closed his book and put it aside. Many aspects of the world scene were touched upon, but at the core of the talks was the wording of a joint announcement on a visit by President Nixon to China. It was important for us not to have the announcement concentrate solely on the issue of Taiwan, as desired by China, but to allow "other issues" to be raised.

Day two began with a visit to the Forbidden City, which I had suggested to Huang Hua as a means of introducing Dr. Kissinger to China's long span of history and illustrious culture. The afternoon's discussions, carried on in the Great

Hall of the People after a Peking duck lunch, became quite hot and heavy. The Chinese raised the question of the alleged US rearmament of Japan, which they regarded as a threat to China. Dr. Kissinger responded that the USSR's powerful military build-up in the region lay behind Japan's rearmament, that it did not threaten China, and that the US nuclear umbrella and military relationship with Japan stabilized the region, turned the Japanese away from a revival of Japanese militarism, and deterred the Japanese from developing their own nuclear capability.

The Korean Peninsula also figured in the discussion, where again Dr. Kissinger pointed out that there was no threat to anyone from the US military presence, which helped to stabilize the military balance. An increase in tensions on the Korean Peninsula was in the interests of neither China nor the US. On Vietnam, each side simply reiterated its position, with Dr. Kissinger drawing attention to the US withdrawal under "Vietnamization."

The Chinese persisted in trying to make Taiwan the centerpiece of the visit, and announcement of a China visit by President Nixon was also a troublesome matter for them. While they were addressing these problems in light of our firm position, we sat around for hours during the second night until our Chinese interlocutor appeared, whether Zhou Enlai or Huang Hua. This delay caused us considerable anxiety and concern.

During the wait Dr. Kissinger took me outside for a stroll beyond the confines of "bugs" to discuss what may have caused the long delay. I surmised that the People's Liberation Army might have had a hand in it, recalling Lin Biao's September, 1965, dissertation "Long Live the Victory of People's War." In retrospect the "Gang of Four" may have also had a hand in the delay.

Finally Zhou and Huang Hua appeared, with Huang being named by Zhou to continue the discussions. By the morning of our departure on July 11 the Chinese had made all the concessions by agreeing to drop any references to Taiwan. The president's visit was set for February, 1972, and the announcement of the visit was to be made by both parties on July 15.

For China, concern over the military threat from the Soviet Union may have outweighed any other factors militating against the Nixon visit. It was certainly evident that the Chinese greatly wanted the Nixon visit to take place. A new beginning for Sino-US relations had begun to emerge. But the Chinese gained considerably, too, as had the US, from the beginning of a new bilateral relationship in which both countries were engaged in difficult negotiations fraught with danger from the Soviet Union. In addition, for China a new basis for looking at the outside world had been established, which would over time bring it more closely into the world mainstream and put it more into a position which China had long desired: being one of the principal arbiters of world affairs.

As for the "Gang of Four," from July 1971 on I have felt that their motivation was not so much ideology as sheer power, and that by taking an anti-US line they believed that they had strengthened their hand in the struggle for the succession to Mao Zedong, who by that time was already beginning to show signs of failing health. I recall seeing a motion picture of Mao meeting with Indonesian Communist Party leader Aidit in July 1965 in which when Mao swung around to face the camera while embracing Aidit, Mao's eyes were glazed and his face was blank. The Kissinger visit to Beijing and the agreement on the terms of the Nixon visit for China occurred while the Vietnam war was still going on with high intensity, indicating that China set a higher value on improving relations with the US than on seeing its "lips and teeth" ally prevail in the conflict.

Once back in the US we went to the "Western White House" in San Clemente. There it was possible to provide a few hours advance warning to key allies about the announcement the president would make on July 15 in a Los Angeles World Affairs Council speech concerning his impending visit to China in February 1972. Alex Johnson had flown in from Washington and had the task of informing the Japanese Ambassador and the ROC Ambassador, while I had all the rest. Above all, I remember the reaction of the South Korean Ambassador, who after a long silence remarked, gracefully, that he hoped the new relationship with China would work out well for the cause of peace. In any event, he said, it was bound to happen some day. We were careful in our remarks to all ambassadors to stress that our relations with their countries would remain unchanged.

Preparing The Presidential Visit

Following the dramatic developments of the secret Kissinger visit to China, the task of making preparations for the next stage, President Nixon's trip to China, lay ahead of us. A multitude of details required attention, such as the timing of the visit, the make-up of the official party, the wording of the joint communique which was to cap the trip, the places to which the president should travel besides Beijing, and the issues to be raised with the Chinese. Among these issues were matters of grand political and military strategy, but also more parochial, working-level concerns, including the Chinese assets frozen by the US at the time of the Korean conflict, and property formerly owned by Americans which had been seized by the Chinese.

Since the multiplicity of details was daunting, I invited my two NSC assistants, Dr. Richard Solomon, formerly of the University of Michigan and the Rand Corporation, and Foreign Service officer Jack Froebe, a "new China hand" trained at State's language school in Taichung, Taiwan, to participate. But their help was still not enough, and consequently Dr. Kissinger agreed to bring State into the planning process and to have a State representative go with him on his next China visit, now set with the Chinese for October 20. The State representative was an old colleague of mine from EA days, Alfred LeSegne Jenkins, Office Director of what was now known as the Office of Chinese and Mongolian Affairs, (CM). Marshall Green, the Assistant Secretary for East Asia and the Pacific, was also brought into the planning.

The State people were promptly put hard to work preparing their own "books," much as we in the NSC had done for the first Kissinger visit, with the exception that eventually there were two sets of books: those prepared by State on the working-level issues, and those drafted by the NSC on he more sensitive matters in Sino-US relations, particularly Vietnam and the Soviet Union. (State's people did venture into this — for them — uncharted territory, but with no road map as a guide.)

All these efforts were played against a background of delicate affairs which could have had a bearing on the president's trip: State's efforts to keep "Red China" out of the UN, or at the minimum preserve a position there for Taiwan, and the mysterious and still-unexplained attempted *coup d'etat* in China by Lin Biao, who had been designated by the CCP's Ninth Party Congress in April 1969 as Mao's successor.

The Lin Biao coup was said by the Chinese to have involved a number of supporters besides Lin, who had plotted with him to blow up a train on which Mao was travelling. When the plot was exposed by Lin Biao's own daughter, those involved fled in an aircraft across the Mongolian People's Republic toward the USSR, but the aircraft crashed in Mongolia under mysterious circumstances, with all aboard killed and burned beyond recognition. The crisis period for China was evidently the first week in September 1971, but the news did not filter out until early October. As a result, the October 1 National Day parade was canceled, and Beijing was put in a state of alert.

Back in Washington, we in the White House and State Department wondered if the planned Kissinger visit to China would be affected. The Chinese, however, went ahead with the trip as projected, requesting only that a public announcement of Kissinger's visit be deferred until October 5. Still, when we actually arrived in Beijing, the signs of tension were plentiful.

My own assignment not long after returning from the trip to Beijing in July was to try a "first cut" at the text of the joint communique to be issued at the end of the Nixon visit. As a starting point, I followed the pattern of other joint communiques which had been issued following a visit by senior foreign dignitaries to Beijing who had met with Chairman Mao, working in such bilateral Sino-US issues as seemed appropriate. This process began about September 1. I was not greatly surprised later to find that what eventually became known as the "Shanghai Communique" bore little resemblance to my initial effort. But as veterans of State and the Federal Service in general know, it always helps to have a piece of paper on hand to use as a starting point.

With all hands connected with the trip working hard, preparations proceeded fairly rapidly, and early October saw us ready to go. Besides Al Jenkins from State, several members of the "advance party" were to go to work out "photo opportunities" and to lay out in a preliminary way the schedule which President and Mrs. Nixon would follow.

The second Kissinger visit to Beijing differed from the first in that the Chinese made a definite effort to publicize it, thus informing the Chinese people that important changes in US-China relations were developing. On the substantive side, more work was done on preparing a joint communique covering the Nixon visit which would be acceptable to both sides.

One subsequent visit to Beijing was considered necessary to tie down logistical matters, such as communications and motorcades, made by Alexander Haig in January 1972. He reported upon his return that Zhou had strongly implied to him that the US should stand firm in Vietnam.

First secret visit to Beijing. Premier Zhou discussing terms for peace with Kissinger: to his right, Holdridge and Lord; to his left, FSO William Smyser. (July 1971).

President at San Clemente, greeting returnees from first secret visit: l/r Hal Saunders, Henry Kissinger, and John Holdridge (carrying The Books).

Kissinger and Foreign Minister Ji Pengfei climb the Great Wall during the second preparatory visit to Beijing, October 1971.

CHAPTER 11

PEACE ACHIEVED!

The beginning of 1972, with the prospect of a climax to all our efforts for peace with China, brought an enormous outburst of energy to my office as well as to my colleagues in State. "The books" of course had to be prepared, but in a different format from anything we in the White House had done before, since it had to be assumed that President Nixon was unfamiliar with many or most of the issues which would be discussed with the Chinese, with the possible exception of relations with Vietnam and with the Soviet Union. Indeed, the main book prepared for the president was in the nature of a tutorial, with analyses of the substantive issues as well as sketches of the major personalities he was likely to meet along with the issues confronting the two sides.

Secretary of State Rogers (plus a sizeable entourage, including Marshall Green) was to accompany the president and Mrs. Nixon on this particular trip. Consequently, State had much the same duties as did we in the NSC, that is, to bring Secretary Rogers up to speed on the issues he was expected to handle and to provide him with the background information he needed.

The difference between the respective books was that the NSC effort was directed mainly at what could be regarded as global or critical policy questions, with State to address bilateral problems. These included the repatriation of American citizens remaining in China. As of early 1972 there were still a few, some voluntarily and some involuntarily), and the question of Chinese assets frozen by the US from the time China had entered the Korean war. On the Chinese side there was American property in China which the Chinese had seized following their defeat of the Kuomintang.

There were, in fact, to be two separate meetings in Beijing. One involved Premier Zhou and the president. The other would be between Secretary Rogers and Foreign Minister Ji Pengfei, in which these bilateral questions were to be dealt with. Fortunately, the Secretary's party included people who were well-qualified to address these questions: Marshall Green, plus Al Jenkins, who had been on the second Kissinger trip to China in October, 1971. Charles Freeman, a Foreign Service officer fluent in Chinese, was to go as an interpreter, both for the president and the secretary.

In addition to the bilaterals, State addressed some of the major elements of foreign policy which we had included in our own books, but though State's papers were duly sent to the NSC and forwarded by me to Dr. Kissinger, whether or not they were passed on to the president is a question which only Dr. Kissinger can answer. (In fact, several weeks later in Beijing I was asked to bring the president's "book" to him from his suite in the guest house, and the only item which I found there was a familiar black-bound volume which we in the NSC had prepared.) As for the bilaterals, Dr. Kissinger and the president were happy to leave these matters for Secretary Rogers to discuss with the Chinese himself.

Our departure from Washington took us first to Hawaii. Following a happy and colorful rest stop we flew on to Beijing. In contrast to Hawaii, our welcome in China (on February 21), while formal and correct, was as chilly as the weather. To be sure, we were met by officials of appropriate rank: Li Xiannian, who as Chairman of the Standing Committee of the National People's Congress of China was as close to being Head of State as China then possessed, and Premier Zhou Enlai, together with their wives. Other senior Chinese officials were present as well, including Foreign Minister Ji. A military honor guard with contingents from each of the three People's Liberation Army services was also lined up adjacent to our aircraft and duly inspected by the president. (The military contingent soon dispersed, and marched away singing a military song well-known to the Chinese: the "Three Main Principles and the Eight Points of Attention.")

The absence of spectators which we had observed at the airport was even more pronounced as our motorcade proceeded toward the city. At every road intersection there were several members of the Public Security Forces posted, who were visibly holding back assorted pedestrians and vehicles in numbers becoming increasingly dense as we approached the center of Beijing. From our car we could see that many necks were being craned to see what was visible of our motorcade, but such curiosity was visibly being discouraged by the Public Security types. We were following a route made familiar in our two previous visits: past the San Li Tun diplomatic quarter (where there actually were some people watching from windows or balconies), a left turn by the Workers' Stadium to Tien An Men Jie, past the Tien An Men, and thence to the Diao Yu Tai guest house area.

The absence of spectators could be attributed to security considerations, but I am more inclined to believe that politics was the cause —there were no diplomatic relations between our two countries, and serious problems, beginning with the Taiwan issue, remained to be resolved. They were not ready to explain to their own public a major about-face. Accordingly, the Chinese leaders saw no reason to be as publicly ostentatious in welcoming President Nixon as they were in private.

The most sensational single element of the visit was the meeting of the two national leaders. In *The White House Years* Dr. Kissinger refers to some of the points which the two leaders discussed, but at the time the staff had no record.

The propensity of President Nixon — and Kissinger — for limiting attendance at high-level talks made it difficult or impossible for the working staff to know what had been said and to follow through with whatever promises, if any, that had been made on either side. (I particularly remember the Nixon-Marcos meeting in Manila in July, 1969, in this respect, where there was no written record and the staff had no way of refuting allegations about the talks which Marcos leaked later on.)

The important factor was the photograph, carried the following day in the *People's Daily*, of President Nixon and Chairman Mao Zedong having their talk in what was plainly Mao's study in the Zhung Nan Hai, the headquarters and residential area of the CCP, located just to the west of the Forbidden City on the edge of the lake which abuts it. Most high-ranking CCP personalities live in this area. Any doubts remaining in the minds of the Chinese people about what was happening in US-PRC relations would have been dispelled by this photograph. It is noteworthy, however, to record that Mao's words, according to Dr. Kissinger, came in bursts as if the Chairman was having physical difficulties. Physical problems on Mao's part, as manifested on this occasion, were to figure importantly in Chinese politics during the next few years in the struggle for his succession.

The second big event for that day was to be the banquet hosted in the evening by Zhou Enlai for the Nixons and their staff members in the Great Hall of the People. In keeping with Chinese hospitality, the entire US party was to be there. As the moment for departure from the Diao Yu Tai approached, we began to assemble from different directions, some from across the lake, the State delegation, and the rest from various parts of the Presidential guest-house, to await the President and Mrs. Nixon and to board our vehicles for the motorcade, already lined up outside.

Bridging the Language Gap

Standing in the hallway of the building were members of the Chinese protocol staff, plus interpreters Ji Qaozhu, Nancy Tang and others who would accompany us to and from the Great Hall. I encountered on the stairs our own American interpreter, Charles Freeman, who expressed concern to me about his ability to do justice to what the president was to say. He explained that he had tried to get a full text of the president's remarks, a hopeless task since the president rarely followed a prepared text but ad-libbed, adding coloration of his own.

The whole banquet was to be given world-wide television coverage, making it a centerpiece of the entire Nixon trip. In typical Nixon style the president could not be expected to adhere to the prepared text which his speech writers had drafted for him. His custom, in fact, was simply to look over the prepared text, and go on from there with remarks which he personally thought were appropriate to the occasion, using very little, if any, of what had been written for him. All we knew was that the president was planning to use some quotes from Mao Zedong's poetry, a collection of which had been made available to him, but we didn't know in advance what poem he would quote or what the correct translation would be.

So there was my friend, Charles Freeman, expected to translate the president's words for literally millions of people world-wide in what was a truly epochal event, but without any real idea of what the president would actually say nor of how Mao's verses could best be translated.

Standing a few feet away was Ji Qaozhu, whose competence as an interpreter had been amply and repeatedly demonstrated during the 1971 Kissinger trips to China. I asked Ji, who was to interpret Chinese to English for Zhou

Enlai, if he was familiar with Mao's poetry and might be able to take on the job of translating from English to Chinese on behalf of President Nixon, in addition to translating for Premier Zhou. Ji didn't bat an eyelash. He said, "of course" to both questions. Our problem was solved. Freeman went on to perform very ably in the bilateral talks between Secretary Rogers and Ji Pengfei.

When the Nixons appeared we boarded our vehicles and proceeded to the Great Hall, where we were met by Premier Zhou Enlai and escorted up several flights of stairs to a grandstand-like structure where we arranged ourselves with our Chinese hosts according to rank for a picture-taking event. In true Chinese style, the background was a painting of pine trees, which to a Chinese audience symbolizes "welcome." We then were escorted into the banquet hall, which was, we were told, capable of handling three thousand guests, but wasn't nearly as crowded on this occasion. There may have been as many as 1000 guests, including high-ranking Chinese and the crowd of press and TV reporters. TV cameras and crews were already in place.

As we entered an army band played traditional American folk tunes and "America the Beautiful." The president and Dr. Kissinger sat at Zhou Enlai's table, and I found myself a few tables away with the Commander of the Beijing Garrison, Wu Zhung (translatable as "militarily loyal") and the Minister of Electric Power.

He began to play with me a Chinese finger game in which the competitors guess the number of fingers each may throw out. The loser would take *mao tai*, a potent drink from Guizhou, where the people of Mao Tai town had succored the weary veterans of the PLA during their famous Long March. When I asked if this traditional Chinese drinking game was still popular, he explained that while this wasn't really revolutionary behavior, old customs persisted.

Zhou Enlai's welcoming speech and the president's response were delivered about midway in the banquet on a stage behind their table which was decorated with the Chinese and US flags. Thanks to Ji Qaozhu, they went off without a hitch, with the TV cameras grinding away. Zhou spoke of the development of Sino-US friendship and of the fact that the president had come such a long distance to inaugurate it, and no elements of controversy such as Vietnam or Taiwan were mentioned.

The president replied in a similar manner, beginning with a quote from a poem by Mao Zedong that a journey of ten thousand *li* begins with but a single step, and that one should "seize the day, seize the hour," looking forward to the continued growth of Sino-US ties and a better future for all. In keeping with Chinese custom, after the speeches Zhou and the president went from table to table to exchange toasts in *mao tai* to each guest. I could see that Zhou was simply touching his lips to the glass and was not drinking — an example which the president followed. The atmosphere in the Great Hall was electric, and surely everyone there, and every TV watcher, must have sensed that something new and great was being created in the Sino-US relationship.

Also in keeping with Chinese custom, once the last dish of the banquet had been served and eaten, the party broke up. Here began what I likened to a stampede of a herd of buffalo across America's prairies in the last century — a horde of guests, all walking swiftly or even running through the vast open spaces of the Great Hall to get to their cars parked in front of the steps of the building, the earlier returnees taking precedence over the later ones in order of departure. Those of us in the official party were thinking first of writing up our collective recollections and then getting some rest after a long, busy day, while the reporters were thinking of stories to be written and deadlines to be met. The Chinese, I suppose, simply wanted to go home.

The Shanghai Communique

While international issues figured in these talks, the main problems were how to address the sticking points left over from previous visits in connection with the Joint Communique. These consisted of the Vietnam question, Taiwan, of course, and the nature of future relations between our two countries. In the February 22 discussions and subsequently, the positions of the two sides began to emerge. There could be no agreed position on Vietnam, or for that matter Laos and Cambodia, since China's ideological principles were so far from our own stand that no bridge was possible. The result was something unique in joint communiques, in that each side laid down its position clearly, e.g. "the US side stated," and "the Chinese side stated," and simply dropped the controversial items to go on to other matters where we could agree.

The next issue to be addressed was Taiwan, and here the language had to be very carefully chosen so that on the Chinese side, as I witnessed the scene, there would be no departure from principle, and on ours, nothing which could be used by opponents of the Sino-US dialogue in the US to claim that Taiwan had been sold out. The best thing going for both sides was the fact that both the CCP and the Kuomintang regarded Taiwan as part of China, and our job was to get the US involvement in Taiwan's defense reduced to a degree which was non-provocative to the Chinese while not abandoning our relationship with Taiwan, and the Chinese to accept a formulation not calling for the use of force in reuniting the island with the rest of China. Finding the exact agreed language occupied a major part of our time.

I was present at the Nixon-Zhou talks as a reporter and adviser, and also checked the Chinese-English translation. My contribution to the Communique was on a relatively simple matter, the maintenance of ongoing ties between the two countries, although of course I had been involved in the discussions of all the other issues. Here I had written what was eventually included in the Joint Communique without change:

> "The two sides agreed that it is desirable to broaden the understanding between the two peoples. To this end, they discussed specific areas in such fields as science, technology, culture, sports and journalism, in which people-to-people contacts would be mutually beneficial. Each side agrees to facilitate the further development of such contacts and exchanges."

These few words nevertheless served as the basis for a large-scale exchange program, in which Chinese students, graduate students in particular, came to the US by the thousands for advanced education, and lesser but still substantial numbers of Americans went to China. Theirs were more in the physical sciences, and ours in the social sciences.

To jump ahead a bit, this paragraph was also the basis on which two US "umbrella organizations," the National Committee on US-China relations and the Committee on Scholarly Exchanges of the National Academy of Sciences, were chosen by the US Government to handle exchanges of people between the two countries, functions which both still perform to this day, although with much less US Government input. Both these bodies were strictly private, but maintained close contact with the US Government, at least in the earlier period of improved Sino-US relations.

The Communique draft included non-controversial elements, including the expansion of bilateral trade. The phrase "normalization of relations between the two countries" occurred for the first time. No date was set for normalization, as both the US and Chinese sides accepted that attaining it would be a difficult process.

Taiwan was an old US friend, and, even though President Nixon could visit China and sign a Joint Communique involving Taiwan, this old friend remained an active player on the East Asian and US political scene. The Chinese showed great restraint and understanding in accepting this fact, but their attitude, particularly that of Zhou Enlai, surely had already been strongly influenced by the words I had written for Dr. Kissinger the preceding July to the effect that the US did not seek "two Chinas, a one China, one Taiwan solution, nor an independent Taiwan" —a position which was reiterated on this occasion. In addition, the US had shown both by word and deed that it had no territorial ambitions in East Asia.

The language in the Communique regarding Taiwan remained a sticking-point, and after dinner at Hangzhou where the president's itinerary had taken him (on February 26) our two negotiating teams found it necessary to meet again.

The crucial sticking points concerned the questions of the possible Chinese use of force against Taiwan to "liberate" the island, and the stationing of US forces in the area, which China regarded both as a threat and a violation of its sovereignty. On the latter element, the Chinese were willing to accept our contention that the US had no territorial ambitions in East Asia, and the US forces in areas other than Vietnam, from which we were withdrawing, acted as a stabilizing factor in the region. This point had been made as far back as Dr. Kissinger's first trip to China in July, 1971.

No US president could leave unaddressed the use of force by China against Taiwan without causing a political explosion back home. For hours those of us at the table attempted to find a formula which would solve the problem, trying variations of wording, only to find that for one reason or another successive versions wouldn't be acceptable to the other side.

What finally emerged long after midnight was another statement by China of its policy that it was the sole legal government of Taiwan and that the island was Chinese territory, etc., following which the US employed a formula acknowledging that "all people [sic] on either side of the Taiwan Strait maintain that there is but one China and that Taiwan is part of China." We then reiterated what we had been saying since July 1971, that we "did not challenge" this position, i.e. China's rejection of "two Chinas," "one China, one Taiwan," or an "independent Taiwan." Significantly, the US statement went on to say, however, that "it reaffirms its interest in the peaceful settlement of the Taiwan question by the Chinese themselves."

Then came the very sensitive operative words, "**With this prospect in mind** (emphasis added), it affirms the ultimate objective of the withdrawal of all US forces and military installations from Taiwan. In the meantime, it will progressively reduce its forces and military installations on Taiwan as tensions in the area diminish." By these words, the US began to take itself out of the Taiwan Strait, both figuratively and ultimately militarily, as an arbiter of Taiwan's future. At the same time, this formula made everything which the US was doing or would do militarily regarding Taiwan contingent on China's maintenance of a peaceful environment in the Taiwan Strait. If China were to insist on its right to use force against Taiwan, and back up its words with military concentrations and/or operations, all bets would be off.

Dr. Kissinger deserves credit for devising this way out of a painful dilemma, but Chinese flexibility helped. In these deliberations, it became evident that the Chinese badly wanted a joint communique which would suit the needs of both parties. They were ready to meet us at least halfway in order to achieve their goal. The Soviet Union did not have a representative sitting at our conference table, but the threat to China of its armed forces stationed along China's borders made it an unseen player.

Issuance of the Shanghai Communique

After our near all-night vigil, which we on the US negotiating team believed would fully satisfy US needs, the presidential party reassembled and went on to Shanghai.

Meanwhile, we on our side were going through a last-minute catharsis. The State contingent had not had the opportunity to inspect the draft of the communique until it was handed to Secretary Rogers on the flight to Hangzhou from Beijing, and having been excluded from all the give-and-take, interposed objections to some of the wording.

There were two elements which above all caught Marshall Green's eye, and through him were carried by Secretary Rogers to the president. The first, in the section dealing with Taiwan, spoke of all "people" on either side of the Taiwan Strait regarding Taiwan as part of China. State objected to the word "people," maintaining that the inhabitants of Taiwan who looked upon the island as their home regardless of the point of origin in China of their ancestors, and regarded themselves as "Taiwanese," would not necessarily agree that Taiwan was part of China. In the event, a satisfactory substitute was found by changing the word "people" to "Chinese," a proposal which was carried to Qiao Guanhua (and certainly through him to Zhou Enlai), which quickly gained Chinese acceptance.

The other point was more difficult. In the original draft of the communique as it was handed to Secretary Rogers, the US reaffirmed continued support for the security obligations which it maintained with Japan, South Korea (the Republic of Korea), the Philippines, SEATO, and ANZUS, but no mention was made of US obligations under its security treaty with the Republic of China on Taiwan.

According to Marshall Green, "this omission would certainly have been seized upon by the world press, and especially by those in the Republican party opposed to the president's trip [Marshall referred in particular to Vice President Agnew and Treasury Secretary John Connally] to charge that the president had sold Taiwan down the river."

According to Dr. Kissinger, when Secretary Rogers raised this matter with the president, an explosion took place, but Dr. Kissinger did, in fact, seek out Qiao Guanhua for a change in the wording of the text. He succeeded with difficulty in obtaining an adjustment which reaffirmed in more general terms the special relationships which existed between the US and several Asian countries with which the US had bilateral military agreements, including the Republic of Korea and Japan, plus advocating a cease-fire between India and Pakistan in Kashmir. No mention of Taiwan or of military agreements was included, however.

Qiao was further told by Dr. Kissinger that the US, in its briefing of the media the next day, would make reference to the treaty with Taiwan. No objection was voiced by Qiao. Once again, Chinese flexibility was being displayed, although this flexibility was undoubtedly being stretched thin. But with these obstacles out of the way, Freeman and I could go over the communique word for word to assure that the Chinese matched the English. Incidentally, we never had problems in this regard with the Chinese, although I was given to understand that our Soviet friends frequently played games of this sort, i.e. not matching the English text with the Russian.

The actual issuance of the communique, which was followed by a media briefing, took place on February 27 in a theater on the grounds of the Jinjiang Hotel (once the Broadway Mansions) where the entire US party was billeted. Both Dr. Kissinger and Marshall Green did the briefing, the latter handicapped by not having been involved in the Communique's formulation.

The task of reaffirming the East Asian defense commitments, including the one with Taiwan, was left to Dr. Kissinger, who faced a question "planted" with a friendly reporter, Kraslow, of the *Los Angeles Times*: "Why did not the US Government affirm its treaty commitment to Taiwan, as the president and you have done on numerous occasions?" Dr. Kissinger replied that this issue was an extraordinarily difficult one to discuss at that time and in that place. He went on to note that "we stated our basic position with respect to this issue in the president's World Report (Annual Report to the Congress on Foreign Policy), in which we said that treaty would be maintained. Nothing has changed on that position." He added that he hoped that this was all he would have to say on this subject. His request was respected.

It was all over but the shouting. The presidential party and the press boarded our respective vehicles for the trip to Shanghai's Hungjiao Airport, but not before the president had personally thanked the entire hotel staff membership for their courtesy by shaking their hands. This made quite a scene before we departed the Jinjiang Hotel, since the

Chinese staff personnel were all lined up along the driveway in order of rank, from cooks to room attendants to bellhops. At the airport there was no formal send-off, but everyone, Chinese officials, US Government officials, airport personnel, Pan Am flight crews, media people, to the number of hundreds, were all mixed together with broad smiles and a vast sense of relief as the President and Mrs. Nixon went up the ramp of Air Force One and waved goodbye. The trip had occurred, had been genuinely successful (even though it took the *Washington Post* and the *New York Times* several weeks to accept this fact), and a new era had definitely been launched in Sino-US relations. The sense of euphoria was pervasive. We who had been involved in the trip in our various capacities boarded our aircraft with a sense of immense accomplishment.

In addition to opening up a new era of Sino-US relations, the Joint Communique also helped to turn China away from its internal problems and encourage it to become a much more positive and outward-looking contributor to the world community of nations — a US objective from the very beginning of our negotiations.

CHAPTER 12

THE VIETNAM ISSUE

We had scarcely returned to Washington before the Shanghai Communique was put to the test. On March 30, coincident with the celebration of Easter in Christian countries, the Vietnamese began a major offensive against the South using regular North Vietnamese troops and attacking strategic areas throughout the northern half of South Vietnam. Quang Tri City fell, and the program of "Vietnamization" was endangered, which may have been one of its main purposes.

Perhaps the Vietnamese were also attempting to disrupt the budding ties between the US and China. The significance of the Shanghai Communique as it affected China's priorities towards North Vietnam must not have been lost on the North Vietnamese.

The Administration, under the personal leadership of the president, reacted vigorously. Restrictions on bombing areas such as the Haiphong dockyards and rail centers in Hanoi were removed, roads and bridges between the Chinese border and the Hanoi/Haiphong area which hitherto had been "off limits" to aerial attack were targeted, and the port of Haiphong was mined by air. (No ship moved in or out of Haiphong Harbor from the date of the mining until the end of the conflict, when the US itself removed the mines as part of the armistice agreement.) The flow of supplies to the North Vietnamese forces was impeded by all these measures.

As the North Vietnamese offensive began, Dr. Kissinger became concerned about the possible adverse political effect of the enhanced US countermeasures on the political relationships which we had just established with China, and on the US-USSR summit meetings which were scheduled to take place in May. Since Vietnam was presumably an ally of both China and the USSR, would the Chinese repudiate the Shanghai Communique? Would the Soviets call off the summit meetings, which were, *inter alia*, expected to discuss arms reductions?

Before the die had been cast and the US forces carried out the orders prepared for them to broaden the air war against North Vietnam and mine Haiphong, on a Saturday afternoon in early April an uncharacteristically disturbed Dr. Kissinger summoned a group of people, myself included, from the NSC and the CIA to the White House situation room. He asked our opinion of what the Chinese and Soviet reactions might be. I believe that he was taken aback to discover that, of all those present only Winston Lord interposed any objections to the stepped–up use of force.

When my turn came, I called attention to the way in which the Chinese in the Shanghai Communique had placed relations with the US on a higher priority than relations with Vietnam, in all likelihood due to concern over its poor relations with the Soviet Union. I said that China, having made such a dramatic change in its long–standing policy in order to establish ties with the US, would probably confine its reactions to expressions of propaganda support for Vietnam but would not otherwise intervene.

My colleague who handled Soviet Affairs, Hal Sonnenfeldt, and I took the position that the Soviets also had a vested interest in keeping the May talks on schedule and would interpose no major difficulties. Failure on the US part to respond vigorously to Hanoi's offensive would have suggested weakness, thus vitiating the balancing role that China wanted the US to play vis-a-vis the Soviet Union. It also could have caused the Soviets to be all the tougher in reaching agreements on crucial matters such as arms control.

My prediction proved to be correct. China unleashed a few cannons of empty rhetoric in the *People's Daily* and other CCP publications about being a "reliable rear area" for Vietnam, but that was it. No perceptible damage was done to our relationship, although I have no doubt that behind the scenes there were those in China who were basically opposed to the opening to the US in the first place and who argued for a more tangible Chinese reaction.

At any rate, the Chinese priorities established in the Shanghai Communique held: relations with the US and movement on the Taiwan question outranked military intervention on behalf of Vietnam. Dr. Kissinger writes in *The White House Years* that he sent Winston Lord to New York to warn China's UN Representative, Huang Hua, to tell Beijing not to interfere. I am not at all convinced that the trip was necessary for that purpose, but as advance word to the Chinese of what we were planning it could have been welcome, if, as Al Haig has alleged, the Chinese virtually endorsed a US victory over Hanoi.

In April and May of 1972 the White House was preoccupied both with the North Vietnamese military offensive and the Moscow summit. But by June the situation in Vietnam had been largely stabilized and the Moscow summit had taken place, both developments to the satisfaction of the White House.

Seemingly undeterred by the stepped–up US military pressures, the Vietnamese kept up their own increased military activities. It was in this atmosphere that Dr. Kissinger was negotiating with Le Duc Tho in Paris in the fall of 1972. In September and October the North Vietnamese actually made some concessions on conditions for ending the war which were accepted by Dr. Kissinger. However, by November the North Vietnamese had backed away from many of these concessions, providing further impetus to the enhanced US military response. The pattern of escalation led eventually to the so-called "Christmas bombings," in which US strategic bombers, the B-52s, were used against such targets as the Hanoi rail marshalling yards. Critics of the "Christmas bombings" may say what they please, but by January 1973 North Vietnamese political conditions for ending the fighting were back to where they had been in September and October.

The Paris accords, concluded on January 27, 1973, ended the full-scale US role in the Vietnam fighting, even though the South Vietnamese (with US military advisers) continued fighting for more than two years.

Aboard Air Force One: The president and Kissinger with Secretary Rogers and Marshall Green en route to China, conferring about the issues (their first group meeting on this subject!)

Overleaves: (1) President and Mrs. Nixon arriving in Beijing, reviewing honor guard with Premier Zhou Enlai. Green and Holdridge at far left. The large sign in Chinese reads "All Oppressed Races Unite to Rise Up!," a slogan later replaced by an exhortation to "increase productivity." (2) Ceremonial welcome in the Great Hall of the People, with Green and Holdridge to the right.

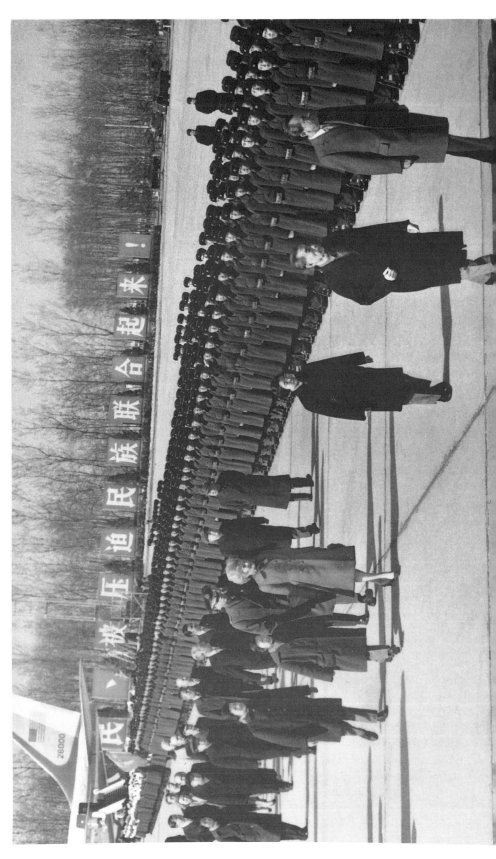

Formal opening of conference for peace. To president's right are Secretary Rogers, Henry Kissinger, Marshal Ye, Marshall Green, Dwight Chapin, Ron Ziegler, Al Jenkins, John Holdridge.

Marshall Green and municipal leaders in Hangzhou, with Holdridge, Buchanan, Scowcroft and Woods.

PART IV

THE STATE DEPARTMENT PERSPECTIVE

by Marshall Green

CHAPTER 13

THE PRESIDENTIAL VISIT TO CHINA

In bringing to an end the 23-year deep-freeze in US-China relations, President Nixon displayed outstanding political courage and a shrewd sense of timing. He seized a moment when Chinese fears of Soviet attack were at a high point to bring about a goal for which we in the Foreign Service had long striven.

But his approach had a serious flaw. The president and an all-too-willing Henry Kissinger handled arrangements for the Beijing summit with a degree of secrecy that kept in the dark key State Department officials —those with an unquestionable need-to-know like Under Secretary Johnson and myself.

Though secrecy was essential in this delicate process, the excessive way it was applied ran serious risks, two of which I helped avert. More fundamentally, it reflected an unwarranted fear of leaks by Foreign Service professionals who, in my experience, are the most trustworthy and leak-proof of all officials involved in the American foreign policy process.

A party of nearly 200 accompanied the president to China, including security, press and administrative aides. The official party numbered 13, ranked as follows: President Nixon, Secretary Rogers, National Security Adviser Kissinger, Presidential Assistant Bob Haldeman, Press Secretary Ron Ziegler, Presidential Military Adviser Brent Scowcroft, Assistant Secretary Green, Presidential Deputy Assistant Dwight Chapin, speechwriter Pat Buchanan, Personal Presidential Secretary Rose Mary Woods, State Department Director of Asia Communist Affairs Al Jenkins, NSC staff member (Foreign Service officer) John Holdridge, and Special

Assistant to Kissinger Winston Lord. But it was clear from our initial seat assignments in the Presidential plane that the White House was going to dominate the show and that the State Department was to take a back seat, literally.

While in Hawaii en route to China I had a useful meeting with Kissinger who gave me the benefit of what he had learned about negotiating with the Chinese, based on his two recent visits to Beijing. Kissinger suggested our meeting in Hawaii since I would be assisting Secretary Rogers in handling what were known as the "counterpart talks" with the Chinese Foreign Minister and his staff. The counterpart talks dealt essentially with specific problem areas like trade, travel, consular affairs, property rights, while leaving broad strategic issues to the top level, namely Mao, Zhou Enlai, Nixon and Kissinger.

"Never," I recall Henry Kissinger saying to me, "use the language of the marketplace in dealing with top Chinese officials. Don't talk about deals or quid-pro-quos. Always talk about principles . . . . That as a matter of principle we are prepared to do so-and-so, and that we would trust that you as a matter of principle would do this or that. The Chinese are real puritans; not like you New Englanders.

"Another thing is that the Chinese have a lot to get off their chests, decades of humiliation at the hands of the imperialist West. The Foreign Minister may well spend two full days sounding off on that subject before he is willing to get into substance. Don't interrupt him. Let him get it out of his system. If you interrupt to rebut him, he'll start all over again, and you'll get nowhere." (He implied that this is what had almost happened to him.)

I recall Henry's emphasis on what was to be a key point in drafting the Shanghai Communique, in which differences of views were clearly set forth followed by areas of agreement. This simple concept was fundamental in reaching agreement. Henry said, "Don't try to pretend differences don't exist when they clearly do. Talk back, remembering that the other side will push and push as long as there is no resistance."

That was Kissinger at his best: astute, articulate, a master of manoeuver, as well as being something of a theoretician, an unusual attribute in the modern American diplomatic experience. But he was also a monopolizer of power, and as long as he was in the White House he lost no opportunity to build his power base at the expense of the State Department, undercutting the Secretary of State. He shamelessly exploited President Nixon's longstanding suspicions and prejudices against career officers (despite our loyalty to all presidents and our high respect for Nixon's extraordinary grasp of strategic issues). This personal lust for power detracted from the national interest when it excluded valuable contributions from institutions designed for the purpose.

For Secretary Rogers, the China trip had many humiliating moments, especially *not* being asked to accompany President Nixon (and Kissinger) to their only meeting with Chairman Mao Zedong. Secretary Rogers was uncomplaining, because he did not want to add in any way to the president's problems.

The crowning achievement of the Nixon China Trip was the final joint statement, the Shanghai Communique, which was to become the charter of our new relationship with China.

Credit for the negotiation of this document must go largely to Henry Kissinger and his Chinese counterpart, Vice-Minister Qiao Guanhua. Henry went through the motions of consulting Secretary Rogers and the rest of the State Department contingent. From time to time Rogers and I would meet with Kissinger, or we would receive sections of the draft communique for our comments, but at no stage did I ever see the entire draft until it was already approved by the president, Kissinger, Rogers and the Chinese leaders.

The first opportunity I was given to read the approved draft was on February 26, the day we left Beijing for a one-day rest stop at the scenic city of Hangzhou before our final day at Shanghai. When we reached our hotel, Secretary Rogers showed me the approved text. I read it rapidly, detecting a major flaw which I immediately drew to Rogers' attention. He agreed with me, and so did Al Jenkins.

The flaw was simply this: although the US reaffirmed in the text of the Communique its support for US security treaty obligations to Japan, the Republic of Korea, the Philippines, SEATO and ANZUS, no mention was made of our treaty obligations to the Republic of China on Taiwan. This would almost certainly be seized upon by the world press, and especially by those in the Republican party who were opposed to the president's trip, to charge that he had sold the Republic of China down the river, that the US had unilaterally terminated without advance notice its treaty obligations to the ROC, and that this could even be interpreted as suggesting to Beijing that it could attack Taiwan without involving the US. (Even top cabinet officials like Vice President Agnew and Treasury Secretary John Connally had privately expressed concern over the president's trip to China.)

Rogers could see my point right away. He, too, remembered how Secretary of State Dean Acheson had come under heavy fire for excluding South Korea from a map showing those areas in East Asia of primary defense concern to the United States. The secretary immediately put in a telephone call to the president who was staying at the nearby government guest house, but he got Haldeman on the phone instead. Haldeman refused to disturb the president who was resting. Besides, he said, the president had already approved the draft.

I was in a black mood that night at the dinner party given in the president's honor by the Hangzhou Revolutionary Committee. Ziegler noted my mood and asked what had happened. When I told him, he evidently then got in touch with Haldeman. Around 2 a.m., John Scali beat on my door and said that "all hell had broken loose in the Presidential Suite." Evidently Haldeman or Rogers had got to the president about the issue, and the president was enraged.

According to Henry Kissinger's memoirs, the president was furious at the State Department for belatedly coming up with a long series of nitpicks about the Communique, and yet failure to correct these nitpicks, the president allegedly feared, might result in the State Department bad-mouthing the Communique. Henry depicted the president as "storming about the beautiful guest house in Hangzhou in his under-wear, swearing that he would do something about that State Department at the first opportunity, a threat he had made at regular intervals since my first interview with him."

Well, of course, there was no series of nitpicks, just one major objection, a point which, amazingly, no one had spotted until I drew it to Rogers' attention, and it is quite possible that the president's fury was directed at Kissinger for having put him on the spot.

The following morning, at breakfast, Secretary Rogers told me that he had managed to reach President Nixon the previous evening to express our concerns. He said he didn't know what the president would do. After breakfast, we left for the airport to go to Shanghai. While proceeding to my plane, Henry Kissinger intercepted me. He was angry about what he termed my "poor-mouthing of the Communique."

For the first time in my three years of association with Henry, I did not hold back. "Since when was the Secretary of State offering constructive criticisms defined as 'poor-mouthing?''' I further reminded him of the constitutional responsibility of the Secretary of State to advise the president — especially on an issue as critical as this, one that could affect the whole outcome of the president's trip.

"But you've been talking to Scali, who has no right to be involved," was Henry's weak retort, to which I replied that Scali had a right to know as press adviser to the president. Henry then did an about-face. He asked if I would join him that evening in briefing the world press at the time of the issuance of the Shanghai Communique. I replied that I would do so if the president so ordered. I was not happy about the prospect of being conspicuously identified with a communique I found badly flawed, and it was left unclear whether that flaw would remain in the communique.

So I arrived in Shanghai in an angry mood until it was revealed to me later in the day that Kissinger had worked out with the Chinese Vice Minister late the previous evening a way of handling the problem I'd raised. I was also told that the president specifically asked that I accompany Kissinger to the press briefing and that I participate to the extent of summarizing what had gone on in the counterpart talks between Secretary Rogers and the Chinese Foreign Minister.

Kissinger never told me specifically what arrangements he had concluded with the Chinese side regarding the critical objection I had raised. During our briefing of a large press gathering in Shanghai at 6 p.m., February 27, it simply took the form of an agreed removal of the offending sentence from the Communique and of Henry's response to an anticipated question from Mr. Kraslow of *The Los Angeles Times* who asked, "Why did not the US government affirm its Treaty commitment to Taiwan, as the president and you have done on numerous occasions?" Kissinger answered that this issue was an extraordinarily difficult one to discuss at that time and place, but then added the key passage: "We stated our basic position with respect to this issue in the President's World Report, in which we said that this Treaty will be maintained. Nothing has changed on that position." Kissinger said he hoped that would be all he would have to say on that subject, and his request was respected.

Thus was adroitly averted what could have been a serious setback. Neither Henry nor the president ever thanked me for my initiative. President Nixon understandably acted as though the event never occurred, while Kissinger took it upon himself to leave history with a self-serving account of the incident — one that is misleading and damaging to the State Department, and one that I am now, many years later, moved to refute.

In any event, this red-letter day concluded on a most pleasant note. I was asked to meet with President Nixon in his hotel room at 10:30 p.m. to discuss the trip which I was about to undertake with John Holdridge, in which we would call on the top leaders of all East Asian and Australasian countries in the course of two weeks to explain American policy in the wake of the Shanghai Communique and to answer questions.

The president was warm and gracious. He gave me instructions as to what I should say about his talks in China: their frankness, their lack of double-talk, that there were no secret agreements or understandings; it was all out in the open as presented in the revealed record. He also urged that I stress America's constancy of purpose and its continuing search, in consultation with our allies, for "finding the right way to stay in Asia," and that under all circumstances we would stand by our commitments.

In assigning John Holdridge to be my assistant, he ensured that we would be in a more authoritative position to answer certain questions relating to the top level talks with

Zhou Enlai which John had attended as an NSC adviser to Kissinger and as an interpreter.

That was the last full day of the president's trip to China. He took off the following morning from Shanghai with all his party (save for John Holdridge and me) direct for Washington by way of Anchorage, Alaska.

For me, the most exhilarating and important moments of the trip all occurred on that last day: my final meeting with Henry Kissinger which turned out so satisfactorily, our joint briefing of the Press (in which he did almost all of the talking and answering of questions), and my final meeting with the president late that evening (February 27).

There was one other event that day which deserves mention. In the afternoon, Premier Zhou Enlai made a personal call on Secretary of State Rogers in his hotel room, which I was asked to join. The subject of my flying direct to Tokyo from Shanghai was raised by Secretary Rogers. Our earlier application to the Chinese government for permission for this flight had gone unanswered. We realized the uniqueness of our application, for no plane of any nation had flown either way between China and Japan in the preceding 23 years. So when Bill Rogers raised the question with Premier Zhou in our hotel meeting, Zhou just smiled and said through his interpreter: "Mr. Secretary, you just go ahead and do what you think is right."

Zhou never gave his permission, but he never refused it either. He thereby established no precedent which someone else could invoke. Zhou was also mindful of how the State Department had been treated by the White House and wished to offset it by this courtesy call. Zhou, in typical Chinese fashion, was keenly aware of the need for officials to save face.

The next day, following President Nixon's departure, I took off in the president's backup plane for Tokyo. Premier

Zhou actually drove down to our plane to say farewell to John Holdridge and me. For the first time, in my hearing, Premier Zhou spoke English: "Goodbye, Mr. Green, have a good trip. Good luck." He knew I faced some difficult moments, especially when I reached Taiwan where I was scheduled to meet with President Chiang Kai–shek. I left China feeling that Zhou Enlai was perhaps the most remarkable of all leaders in terms of his broad command of world events combined with his extraordinary attention to detail.

Communicating the Message

Arriving in Tokyo on February 28, John Holdridge and I were met by my wife and by special assistant, Paul Cleveland. We four were to make the long journey from Tokyo to Seoul, Taibei, Manila, Saigon, Phnom Penh, Vientiane, Bangkok, Kuala Lumpur, Singapore, Jakarta, Sydney, Canberra, Wellington and back to Washington.

The most challenging talks we had were in Tokyo and Taibei. As *The New York Times* put it on the day of our arrival in Tokyo: "The Japanese press is beside itself in frustration — and the government is not far behind — that Japan's overtures toward normal government relations with Beijing have been spurned; while President Nixon has been welcomed. China professes to fear revived Japanese militarism and Japanese economic hegemony in Asia."

My meetings with Prime Minister Sato and Foreign Minister Fukuda were nevertheless warm and friendly, based on many years' acquaintance, even though they were under criticism in Japan for the way the US had overtaken Japan in the race to Beijing. They were also anxious for "inside" information regarding what had transpired in the summit meetings in Beijing beyond what was already announced.

This placed me on a bit of a spot because I had not been directly involved in the top-level negotiations with Zhou, a fact known to the Japanese press. On the other hand, Kissinger and President Nixon had given me background and guidance, and John Holdridge had attended most of the summit meetings.

The Japanese government had already made favorable official statements about the Shanghai Communique before our arrival in Tokyo. The government's statements after my departure would indicate that our talks in Tokyo had gone well in the sense of removing suspicions that there were secret deals in Beijing, perhaps involving Japan, in reaffirming our defense commitment to Taiwan, and in suggesting that we had no desire to beat Japan in any race toward diplomatic recognition of Beijing.

I remember most vividly two experiences in Korea. One, the 90-minute grilling we had from the Korean Foreign Minister with regard to every detail of the president's China Trip, plus our assessment of each detail's implications. In contrast, my friend (and former foe) President Park Chung Hee expressed great concern about my personal safety when visiting Taiwan in view of the strongly adverse reactions he anticipated there.

I accordingly prepared careful talking points during the Seoul-Taibei flight that I later checked with Ambassador McConaughy in Taibei before our meetings with top Taiwanese officials. President Chiang Kai-shek refused to see us, but his able, level-headed son, Chiang Chingkuo, who was premier at the time and later president of the ROC, was our gracious, albeit dismayed host. I assured the premier and foreign minister that, while we had modified our policy toward Beijing, we had not changed our policy toward the ROC with which we continued to have diplomatic relations and a defense commitment. We also expected to do even more to encourage trade and investment in Taiwan. In the Shanghai Communique we made explicit our view that there is but one China, rejecting any suggesting that we favor a two-China policy or a one-China, one-Taiwan policy. We do not pretend, I added, to know how the Taiwan issue will eventually be settled. This is a problem to be resolved by the Chinese on both sides of the Taiwan Strait. We only insist on the issue being resolved peacefully.

After a busy day of meetings in which these themes were stressed, and many questions answered by John Holdridge and me, I said to the foreign minister at our final meeting that I hoped his government would not convey an impression of dismay and bitterness over President Nixon's China initiative. That would only give satisfaction to those who are enemies of the ROC and instill fears on the part of Taiwan's business contacts. The ROC has many strong friends in the US and elsewhere, and it must remain that way.

Subsequently, our Embassy reported that reactions in Taiwan remained skeptical but the "GRC leaders were impressed with Green's reaffirmation of the defense commitment and most interested in his comment that he believed Beijing is prepared to accept the status quo in Taiwan for an indefinite period. Most important of all, the GRC leaders did not engage in a further public quarrel with the US. Private comments also indicated relief and a shift from earlier sharp criticism." With the help of Walter McConaughy and John Holdridge my difficult mission to Taiwan succeeded.

Our next stop after a scary flight through a tropical electrical storm was Manila, a scene of utter confusion. Mrs. Marcos was taking off for Beijing just as we landed. Our ashen-faced ambassador, Hank Byroade, explained that Mrs. Marcos was looking for new relations with Beijing, now that the US had allegedly changed its policy. Byroade also said that I was being served with a subpoena to appear the following day before the Philippine Senate to answer questions about "how the US was reneging on Its Two China policy," which Foreign Minister Romulo had thought we were pursuing. The Philippine press reaction was shrill and irrational, urging that since the US had jettisoned Taiwan the Philippines should now negotiate a deal with Beijing.

According to the Embassy's telegraphic reports of my 36 hours stay in Manila, my meetings with Marcos, Romulo, the Philippine Senate, the press, etc. had been "indispensable in halting the snowballing erosion in Philippine confidence in US Asian policy."

Our meetings in Vietnam, Cambodia and Laos were held in a calmer atmosphere and went off without incident, except for President Lon Nol's absence (for medical treatment in the US). I had little regard for him anyway and was glad to have my meetings instead with Sirik Matak, the Foreign Minister, a wise and courageous man.

The King of Thailand, reflecting the sentiment of his government and people, expressed to me profound skepticism of PRC intentions and of US ability and preparedness to deal realistically with the Chinese. However, on our departure from Bangkok after long separate meetings with the king, the prime minister, the foreign minister, the National Executive Council, the SEATO secretary general, and the press, the Thai government released a statement describing our talks as "most satisfactory to both sides while at the same time creating excellent mutual understanding." The usually critical leading newspaper *The Nation* said I had done a "superb job in allaying suspicions." During my talks in Thailand I was in a position to provide private assurances that Beijing was likely to reduce, and possibly terminate, material support for Communist insurgents operating in Thailand.

Our stops in Kuala Lumpur and Singapore were relatively uneventful but entirely satisfactory.

Indonesia posed a special problem in terms of Indonesia's deep suspicions of the Chinese, who were regarded as co-conspirators with the Indonesian Communist Party in assassinating 6 of Indonesia's top 8 generals in the aborted coup of September 30, 1965. On the other hand, President Suharto, Foreign Minister Malik, and the Army leaders welcomed Nixon's China trip as offering hope for peace and stability. Press coverage emphasized my assurances that there had been no change in US commitments and no secret deals.

In Australia there was no need to explain or justify the president's trip to China. It was widely accepted as a sensible move. However, Australia posed an interesting challenge since the leader of the Labor Party opposition, Gough Whitlam (who was Prime Minister during my assignment to Australia 1973-75), had adopted the position that Australia should now establish relations with the PRC. The leader of the Country Party was similarly interested in early recognition of Beijing as giving Australia a diplomatic advantage in selling wheat and other farm products to the huge China market. I found myself in something of a quandary in justifying the president's opening to China on the one hand and advising caution regarding any Australian move to recognize Beijing on the other. All I could do was suggest that Australia might be best advised to adopt a wait-and-see policy before any moves to break relations with Taiwan in order to recognize Beijing.

New Zealand, our last stop, was delightfully relaxing. After a useful 2-hour talk with Prime Minister Marshall and Foreign Minister Holyoake, the prime minister suggested that we conclude our talks on the Heretaunga Golf Course, which we did. Sir Keith Holyoake told the press that my "briefing was the best one he had ever heard in his life."

This was a pleasant note on which to end a trip that had covered a dozen countries in three weeks.

In looking back on this trip, my wife remarked on the wisdom of President Nixon in entrusting this mission to Foreign Service officers who were not only well-known personally to leaders of the Western Pacific region, but who were seen by them as having no political axes to grind.

On our return to Washington, I reported to the White House before going on the nation-wide NBC program *Meet the Press*. The president, when I met with him on March 23, along with Al Haig, Kissinger's deputy, and John Holdridge, was anxious that I play down the Taiwan aspect as much as possible in my *Meet the Press* appearance. He did not want me to make any headlines — and I did not disappoint him in that regard. Al Haig called me up after my NBC performance to say, "They didn't lay a glove on you," but I fear it was a lackluster TV performance, given my instructions.

US policy toward China naturally had an impact on our relations with Japan. Prime Minister Sato resigned in mid–1972 and was replaced by Prime Minister Tanaka who had already announced his intention to negotiate later that year with the Chinese on normalizing Tokyo's relations with Beijing. On August 30, 1972, I accompanied President Nixon to Hawaii where Nixon and Tanaka met for the first time, largely to get to know each other and to discuss issues of concern.

On our flight from San Clemente on Air Force One to Hawaii, there was a long meeting in the president's cabin attended by the president, Secretary Rogers, Kissinger, Under Secretary U. Alexis Johnson and myself, in which Alex did most of the talking. He had previously been our Ambassador to Japan and felt strongly that President Nixon and Kissinger had unnecessarily affronted the Japanese in the way we had suddenly shifted our policy toward Beijing in 1971–72 without adequate consultation or proper notification of Japan.

Clearly, Prime Minister Tanaka was now going to move rapidly, under strong internal Japanese political pressure, to normalize Tokyo-Beijing relations. Some concern was expressed in our Air Force One meeting that Tanaka might normalize on terms adversely affecting US interests, but President Nixon seemed surer than the rest of us that Tanaka and Zhou would act responsibly and that we should not press the Japanese on this issue at our forthcoming meeting in Hawaii.

Since the president's main meetings there with Tanaka were strictly private and separate from the plenary talks, I have no way of knowing whether China-Japan issues were discussed. But, in any event, when Tanaka did go to Beijing several weeks later, he was evidently under no pressure from the Chinese to accept terms that would create difficulties in US-Japanese relations. In fact, China seemed to be at pains not only to improve relations with Japan, but also with the United States, and between Japan and the United States.

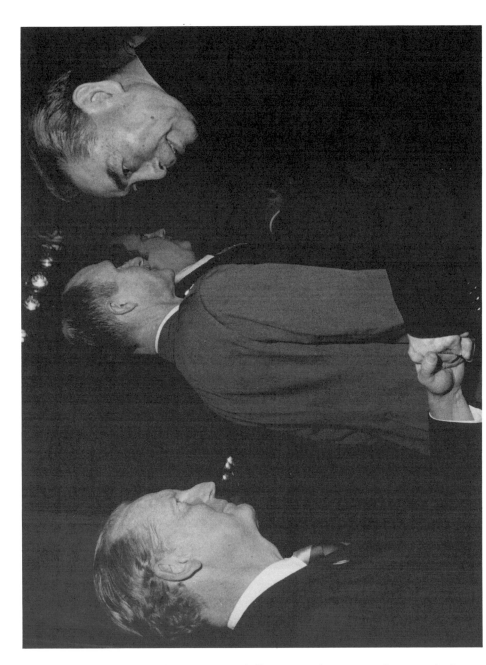

Premier Zhou Enlai greets Marshall Green. *The Los Angeles Times* had earlier commented, "Though divided by 18 years and half a world, Zhou and Green had a common objective in better US-China relations."

Japanese Prime Minister Sato and Assistant Secretary Green discuss the Nixon visit to China and policy implications for US-Japan relations. This was the first stop on a 13-nation visit by Green and John Holdridge.

The King of Thailand receives Green for a discussion of the negotiations between the US and China as they effect Southeast Asia.

Green and Holdridge reporting to President Nixon on results of their Asian tour and Green's impending appearances before Congress and *Meet the Press*.

CHAPTER 14

A RETROSPECTIVE OVERVIEW

A major unforeseen and constructive result of the president's China initiative was that it led, within the year 1972, to a constructive relationship among the world's most powerful nation, the world's most populous nation and the world's most economically dynamic nation — all three of them having been at war with each other at some point earlier in this century.

When future historians contemplate the events of this century, few things will stand out more prominently than the interface between China and the United States. Barbara Tuchman's *Stillwell and the American Experience in China* captures all the frustrations of our war–time allied relations when she writes in her final sentence: "In the end, China went her own way, as if the Americans had never come."

Thereafter, for over two decades, US relations with mainland China remained in a deep freeze. There was a brief period between late 1961 and early 1964 that offered some hope that relations might thaw a bit due to Chinese reactions to the excesses of the Great Leap Forward and to initiatives from the American side to enter into a more civil discourse with China. This period was marked by US efforts to relax certain restrictions on American travel to, and trade with, China. It was also marked by US pressures, known to Beijing, to restrain our Chinese allies on Taiwan from raids against the mainland, especially during the period of economic and social unrest resulting from the collapsed Great Leap Forward.

However, there was no evidence of Beijing's willingness to relax tensions with the US even during the 1961-64 period. The US was nevertheless able to demonstrate that it was Chinese, not US, policy that was principally responsible for the continuing deep freeze in our relations.

The Chinese government was obviously averse to any gradual improvements in its relations with the US. As I pointed out at Princeton in mid-1965: "Chinese Communist leaders have remarked that when the time comes to improve relations with the US 'this will come all at once, inasmuch as to improve relations piecemeal would have a harmful effect on the Chinese people's revolutionary fervor'."

Partly as a result of the setback to China caused by the aborted Communist coup in Indonesia in 1965, China entered into another dark period of left-wing fanaticism known as the Cultural Revolution which did not abate until 1969. Intensified efforts were made by China during that period to cast the US in the devil's role in order to whip up mass fears of an external threat and thereby achieve national cohesion.

A major reversal of Chinese strategic policy occurred in the period 1969-71, brought on by increasing Chinese nervousness over Soviet intentions. The Soviet invasion of Czechoslovakia in 1968, followed by the rapid build-up of Soviet military power in Siberia, especially in disputed areas along the Chinese frontier, created an atmosphere of war-panic in China. Air raid shelters were built on a massive scale. A CIA estimate of October 1969 placed the chances of a Soviet effort to knock out China's nascent nuclear weapons factories at about 1 in 3. Meanwhile, ever since Khrushchev came on the scene, China had been nervously observing US-Soviet relations and was increasingly concerned that China might face US-Soviet collusion. It was against this background —plus the growing influence of Zhou Enlai and the pragmatists —that President Nixon's initiative had a realistic hope of success.

Why did the president take this extraordinary initiative on China? Certainly it was out of line with the thinking of many in the Republican party. It also involved a lot of risks:

- secret preparations might leak to the press,
- the highly publicized summit meeting might fail,
- there might be bad reactions in Japan, Korea, Taiwan or elsewhere.

Moreover. he was undertaking this trip at a time when the war in Vietnam was raging and when the US was suffering heavy casualties at the hands of an enemy supported by Beijing. Finally, his approach to China could be seen as a bit premature. Why not wait until Mao passed from the scene — which seemed fairly imminent?

The very fact that the president took all these risks underlines the great importance he attached to a US-China rapprochement. As he said to me on one occasion: "We simply cannot go on indefinitely in a hostile relationship with one quarter of mankind, especially as the PRC grows in military power." There was a need to move promptly at a time when the Chinese leaders were fearful of a Soviet attack and when we could not allow the Soviet Union to take Sino-US hostility for granted in its policy calculations.

The president also had sound internal political reasons for his China initiative. It was widely popular in the US, especially in academic, press and other circles critical of our role in the long, bloody, fruitless war in Vietnam. For many months, China took the headlines away from Vietnam. It cast US foreign policy in a positive light during a critical year for the Nixon Administration.

President Nixon had a strong sense of the mark he would leave on history. That was evident from my first meeting with him in Jakarta, with all his notetaking and tape-recording of conversations. China's affirmative response to Nixon's initiatives related overwhelmingly to its fears of Soviet aggressive intentions and of possible Soviet-US collusion against China. But other factors were also undoubtedly involved. One of them was the perceived advantage to Beijing in having closer ties between Beijing, Washington and Tokyo, both in economic terms and in terms of better ensuring that Japan's military capabilities would remain limited and confined to Japan's self-defense through its defense ties with the United States. This point came through to me loud and clear in a conversation with a top Chinese official in Beijing during the Nixon visit. The Chinese have long memories, and surely one of the most painful of these memories is Japan's harsh occupation of North China and its half-century colonization of Taiwan.

President Nixon was criticized for failing to recognize Japanese sensitivities in the sudden announcement of his trip to China. For years the Japanese had followed the American lead on China policy, even though they were anxious to get into the Chinese market through early recognition of the Beijing government. It had been the nightmare of at least one top Japanese official that he would wake up one morning to find the Americans in Beijing and the Japanese left in the lurch.

It would have been possible to soften the blow to Prime Minister Sato and his government had President Nixon sent a personal emissary like Ambassador U. Alexis Johnson, who was well known and trusted in Japan, to explain in the greatest secrecy the president's initiative about a day in advance of its announcement. This would have given Prime Minister Sato time to ready his public response, while underlining our respect and understanding for Japan's special interests in this important strategic move.

That the president decided against such a move related to his concern that Sato would have felt obligated to share that secret information with key government party associates, possibly leading to an embarrassing leak shortly before the president's appearance on TV to announce to the world his plan to visit China.

As the then Under Secretary of State, U.Alexis Johnson, has said in his memoirs (*Right Hand of Power*, p. 554) the matter could have been handled in a manner which would have avoided such a risk.

I sensed that both Nixon and Kissinger compared the Japanese leadership unfavorably with the Chinese, seeing the Japanese as preoccupied with economic issues while the Chinese leaders thought in Nixon–Kissinger global strategic terms. It was not until Nixon returned to Washington from China that I learned that his obsession with keeping his China initiative secret was not, as alleged by Nixon, out of consideration for the wishes of the Chinese, but for his own.

Some time after the president returned from Beijing, I suggested through Under Secretary Johnson and Henry Kissinger that President and Mrs. Nixon might show their respect for Japan (and make amends for the Nixon shocks) by flying to Alaska to greet Their Imperial Majesties, the Emperor and Empress of Japan, who were stopping over at Anchorage for refueling en route by polar flight to Europe. This was the first time in history that any reigning monarch of Japan was to set foot on foreign soil — and it was to be American soil. President Nixon took warmly to the idea (which he probably assumed was Kissinger's) and Japanese reactions were highly favorable.

A black mark on the president's China trip was the shabby way he treated his old friend and loyal supporter, Secretary of State William Rogers. American presidents in recent memory have had a tendency to rely considerably more on White House staff than on government departments, but in Nixon's case it was carried to extremes, abetted by a long-standing distrust of the State Department, including the Foreign Service.

It was a curious coincidence that my 17 consecutive years in dealing with US China policy should have started and ended by working for two right-wing Republican lawyers, John Foster Dulles and Richard Nixon. Both started out their public careers as anti-Communist zealots with simplistic solutions to international issues, and both ended their careers as international statesmen.

It remained for President Nixon to shake the extended hand of Zhou Enlai in 1972 in dramatic contrast to Dulles' refusal to do so in Geneva in 1954. As President Nixon wrote in 1983 (*Leaders*, p. 218) "Both men and events contributed to the diplomatic breakthrough that was formalized by the Shanghai Communique. The one man who deserves the primary credit was Zhou Enlai."

US–China relations had come a long way.

USLO Chief George Bush commenting to Inspector Stokes and Deputy Chief Holdridge on how, metaphorically, the "Great Wall" is being breached by good will and cooperation. (October 1975)

ZHOU ENLAI: PEACEMAKER

The decisive stand taken by Zhou for responsible internationalism came from a lifelong commitment. He asserted this position early, when it was not the party's dominant position. In 1946, as the chief CCP representative to General Marshall's tri–partite commission which sought a negotiated settlement of the civil war, he convinced Marshall by repeated conciliatory positions that he wanted the American effort to succeed. In 1950, he originated a message to the US warning of Chinese imminent military intervention in Korea, when Mao wanted the US forces to plunge ahead into a trap.

During the disasters of the early 1960's he was not able to deflect Chairman Mao from his radical policies, but neither could anyone else. He survived in Mao's inner circle, when many colleagues perished.

With the physical and political decline of Mao, perhaps beginning in 1965, he struggled for and gradually achieved the succession to power. He first out–maneuvered Lin Biao, Mao's formally designated successor, who had spoken for exporting revolution and against cooperation with the US. By 1971 Lin died in flight. Then Zhou overcame the radicals who cloaked themselves in Mao's political aura. By the time of the Secret Visit he was clearly in full control of Chinese foreign policy. Of course Zhou was greatly aided by the nakedness of Russia's military threat, but it must have taken extraordinary skill and daring to mobilize the Chinese leadership to reverse Mao's strategic tilt toward Moscow.

As this book shows, Zhou employed his growing stature to redirect Chinese policy towards political and economic participation in the comity of nations. Indeed, he took substantial risks in doing so before he had consolidated his political position. He began by directing Chinese responsiveness at the Warsaw talks and then put himself on the line with a truly decisive step. He sent a hand–written letter to President Nixon, delivered on December 8, 1970, suggesting a high–level visit to China for discussions of Taiwan. He responded to Nixon's warm rejoinder not only with an expressed willingness to discuss other issues as the US desired but also with an invitation to President Nixon personally to head the US delegation.

When the visit materialized Zhou led the Chinese side to agreement, made sure that divisions on the US side were mollified by his attentiveness, and continued a steady course toward normal relationships in subsequent dealings, despite the war in Vietnam.

Though struck by cancer early in 1973 he persevered to keep China's policy on course, When he died, his policies were pursued and expanded by his eventual successor, Deng Xiaoping, so that the world still benefits from his legacy.

(W.N.S.)

PART V

OUTLOOK

CHAPTER 15

NORMALIZATION, POPULATION, TRADE AND INVESTMENT

Achievement of what amounted to a peace with China opened the way for progress on a wide range of strategic, political, economic and social issues beyond the scope of this book. We close with summary observations on topics of our continuing individual involvement.

NORMALIZATION

by John H. Holdridge

John Holdridge was a principal in the painstaking task of seeking normalization as Deputy Chief of the US Liaison Mission in Beijing, first with David Bruce and then George Bush. After service as Ambassador in Singapore he became Assistant Secretary for East Asia (1981-82). Since retiring from the Service he has been working on a detailed study which he plans to entitle *Zheng Chang Hua: Normalization of Diplomatic Relations between the US and the People's Republic of China.*

After the spate of high-level *ad hoc* visits to China, it was essential to establish resident representation. In May 1973 China and the US opened missions in each other's capital. The US post in Beijing, called a "Liaison Office"(USLO) enjoyed diplomatic immunities, secure communication, individual travel, and most importantly, access to China's top leaders. Moreover, by residing in Beijing USLO personnel had a vantage point for assessing developments in China at close hand. The only limitations on USLO's diplomatic status was that the USLO chief did not participate in the biannual visits to various areas of China organized by

China's Foreign Ministry. Nor did he attend banquets in Beijing's Great Hall of the People in honor of visiting VIPs.

Shortly after the USLO's establishment American business began to move into China. The first big contract was won by the Kellogg-Pullman Corporation for construction of nitrogen fixation plants. The Boeing Corporation and RCA soon thereafter also won large contracts. From this auspicious start, after a period of experimentation, trade and investment has flourished in the manner recounted later in this chapter.

On the strategic side, China has kept to the terms of the Shanghai Communique in peaceful settlement of the Taiwan question by the Chinese themselves. There has been no Chinese military build-up along China's coastline opposite Taiwan for these many years since the Shanghai Communique. That restraint continued even when President George Bush authorized the sale of $6 billion worth of F-16 aircraft to Taiwan in order to win Texas, where the F-16s are made, during the 1990 Presidential elections. In my opinion, this sale flagrantly violated the terms of the Joint Communique of August 17, 1982 on Arms Sales to Taiwan, which calls for a gradual reduction in such sales. The Taiwan Relations Act of 1979 authorizes the US to respond to what we regard as Taiwan's military "needs," but in the absence of a palpable Chinese threat to Taiwan, how can we justify a sales increase of that magnitude?

China has been responsible in exercising its power in the UN Security Council. Its support or abstention on resolutions concerning the US-backed coalition's use of force against Iraq made it possible for operation Desert Storm to take place. Conversely, China's present reluctance to go along with the US and other countries in agreeing to impose sanctions on North Korea for non-compliance with International Atomic Energy Agency inspections of certain North

Korean nuclear facilities and activities has slowed the sanction process down. China obviously is a big player in this drama, a fact which the US must take into account.

The same is true for other strategic issues such as non-proliferation of nuclear weapons and strategic missiles. While China has proved somewhat difficult on certain aspects of these problems, the situation would have been far worse had there not been a reasonably friendly China with which the US could deal. That is particularly true in the light of China's huge population, the size of its armed forces, and its strategic geographic location.

China's military capabilities are growing, notably its program for a blue-water navy capable of enforcing its claims to the supposedly oil-rich Spratly Islands in the South China Sea and for acquiring high-technology aircraft from Russia for its air force.

Politically, China regards itself as a member of, and possibly the natural leader of, the Developing World. It has improved its relations with the countries sharing its location in East Asia, and has maintained ties with some of the world's "rogue states," including Iraq, Iran, and Libya. Obviously, China wields influence in areas which may be real trouble spots for the US and the West in the years to come. Equally obviously, it behooves the US not to alienate beyond redemption its current working relationship with China, and in fact, to build upon this foundation in the future.

My own belief is that it will be possible for the US to maintain and improve good working relations with China if the US treats China as an equal, and accords it the degree of respect to which the Chinese leaders and people believe it is entitled as the inheritor of a history and culture dating back well over 3000 years. As the Chinese say, "equality and mutual benefit" lie at the bedrock of its relations with other countries, including the US. The US would be wise to bear Chinese sensitivities in mind. Resolution of the human rights question in China can take place under such circumstances, so long as the question is discussed quietly with the Chinese, and neither made a major issue in our bilateral ties nor discussed openly in the harsh light of media publicity. The starting point for all these elements is unquestionably the Shanghai Communique.

POPULATION

by Marshall Green

Marshall Green has closely followed population developments in China since he resigned as Ambassador to Australia in 1975 to become the Department's first coordinator for Population Affairs, concurrently chairing the National Security Council's *ad hoc* Task Force on World Population and heading the US delegation to the United Nations Population Commission. After retirement in 1979 he served as consultant to the Department on Population Problems and chaired its advisory panel on Indo-Chinese refugees. He was also a Director of the National Committee on US-China Relations and a member of the Asia Society's President's Council. He continues to write and speak about US-China policy, visiting China and Hong Kong frequently, largely on population issues.

The most fundamental long-term problem facing China is to stabilize and control its huge population, 1.2 billion, more than a fifth of the human race. It is currently growing at the rate of 135 million every decade.

During my visit to China in 1985 as a guest of the State Family Planning Commission (SFPC), I was struck by the overcrowding and congestion of China's cities, the high levels of air and water pollution, and by the oft-cited facts that China had 25 to 33 percent as much cropland as the world per capita average, 25 percent as much fresh water, 50 percent as much grassland and 12 percent as much forested land. Its population had already passed the one billion mark and seemed certain to grow by at least a half billion more, despite the rigorous one child family norm announced by Beijing in 1979.

One of the principal reasons for my trips to China in 1985 and 1986 was to study the degree to which China was guilty of coercive practices in its family planning program.

I saw no direct evidence of such practices, although my hosts conceded that they did occur despite government efforts to stamp them out. They declared physical coercion, especially relating to sterilization and abortion, was an "intolerable crime."

Meanwhile, ardent US right-to-life opponents of family planning used China's one-child family norm program and its reported excesses to attack US population assistance programs in general and US contributions to the UN Population Fund in particular, since the Fund was supporting China's family planning program (though not China's policies). As a result, the Reagan and Bush administrations suspended US aid to the Fund, a policy that was reversed by the Clinton administration.

In retrospect, it would appear that the draconian one-child family program began to ease after 1983, with more and more exceptions given in rural and fishing communities where the need for a son to carry on the family business was essential.

Today, the combined effect of massive internal migration, decentralization of authority and considerable corruption (involving officials at all levels) makes it difficult to judge the program's effectiveness. But Beijing remains firmly committed to lowering birth rates, laying down rules of conduct and setting quotas for provinces and counties while leaving program implementation to the *dan wei* (work units).

Overall, the prospects for stabilizing the population of China within the range of 1.5 to 1.7 billion during the 21st century look good thanks to its family planning program plus the supportive effects of urbanization, industrialization and economic development, consumerism, and the communications revolution. Especially in the cities, childbirth is postponed until young couples amass worldly goods and achieve a better life style. China's urban population is now close to 30 percent of the total, after being less than 20 percent.

Nevertheless, China's population, thanks to past growth momentum, now seems likely to increase by the equivalent of twice the population of the United States. This carries ominous environmental overtones for China, the region and the world, bearing in mind China's industrial growth, rising consumption levels, and heavy dependency on its vast coal reserves. Emission controls and the development of alternative energy sources will be imperative.

China's projected population growth also connotes an intensification of large-scale migratory flows, both internal and external with the US as a promising goal, through illegal channels if necessary.

Had China tackled its population problem earlier in the century, it would have been able to deal with it through more conventional and acceptable measures. However much one may regret the draconian character of China's current program to combat population growth, it was and is in the fundamental long-term interest of mankind that China reach its objective.

This is well appreciated in Asia; less so in the US.

194

TRADE AND INVESTMENT

by William N. Stokes

After inspecting US conduct of relations with the PRC in 1975, including the Guangdung Trade Fair and the US Liaison Mission in Beijing, Stokes resigned from the Service to become director of Third World projects for A.T. Kearney, Inc., a multi-national consulting firm. With Kearney he led numerous consulting teams in China, assisting local industries to qualify for world market entry and foreign firms to succeed in manufacturing under the special circumstances in China. He is principal author of *Manufacturing Equity Joint Ventures in China*, an experience guide based on results achieved by 72 international firms.

Assessing China's abject poverty in 1971, after a generation of absolute centralization, Mao's successors wanted to explore how free markets and world trade might produce prosperity on the mainland as in overseas Chinese communities like Taiwan, Hong Kong, and Singapore.

Soon after normalization of diplomacy with the US, Deng Xiaoping proclaimed an "Open Door" for foreign trade and investment in China. Laws permitting the formation of joint ventures between foreign and Chinese firms soon followed. Foreign firms rushed to test the possibilities. While limiting their initial commitment in view of the practical difficulties, they created a new climate of modernized business practices in thousands of partnerships with Chinese firms, which were encouraged to do so by the government through the granting of many new procedural freedoms and rights of independent business judgment.

And likewise in the countryside. In Deng's home province of Szechuan, an experimental award of private land tenure to farmers produced astonishing increases in agricultural output. The practice became national, and Mao's commune system dissolved. Output so expanded that the large wheat imports from the US until 1980 became unnecessary. Today China has a virtually balanced foreign trade in food,

China is the first Communist state to have completely transformed its agriculture from collective to private operation *and* now to have developed an important export engine of private industry. Industrial success (unlike Japan's more insular miracle) has been achieved through international equity investment and management of joint ventures. This form of organization promotes assimilation of international practices and attitudes among the Chinese participants, contrary to China's traditionally inward-looking social tendency. Individual initiative and skills development are rewarded, with cultural influences amounting to a social revolution.

Deng's formula has been "One China, Two Systems," but the Socialist system is in full retreat under competition with the market-oriented sector. The Chinese treasury has manifest interest in phasing out the huge subsidies for inefficient State enterprises, which have fallen to less than half of the industrial sector. As alternative employment is found for its subsidized labor, the Socialist sector is likely to diminish further. Nor can it count on continued favor from the political leadership, judging from the current elevation to national power of technocrats well-versed in market economics.

China's economy is already the world's third largest, and it is the fastest growing, both as an export market and overall. Today foreign businesses are contracting to commit over $50 billion of investment in China per year, five times the total in 1991.

A comparable future rate of growth seems predictable. China, only now recovering from the educational holocaust of the Cultural Revolution, will soon manifest internally the technological innovation in which Chinese in the US have been such leaders. Chinese management has made tremendous progress from its intimate association with joint ventures. And China is no longer wholly dependent upon foreign capital, given its favorable balance of trade today. When China exploits and exports the huge petroleum deposits on its Western frontier, in the Tarim Basin, it will have another impressive engine of economic growth.

The imminent reunion of Hong Kong with China will combine two economies with favorable and growing balances of payment, cementing the symbiosis of trade and industry which has benefitted both parties. Indeed, China has invested heavily in creating miniature Hong Kongs in the free trade zones which have sprung up all along the coast. The current state of investor confidence in Hong Kong suggests that the reunion will not kill the goose that has been laying golden eggs. There are of course potential impediments:

inflation (which the current regime has always curbed when overheating became severe):

corruption (vexing to modern business practice, but mainly confined to the waning public sector influence over allocation of materials, supplies and transportation),

infrastructure weaknesses (which have high priority for remedial investment), and

governmental succession, the great unknown, which could undo everything.

So, what about political evolution? The 1990 reform movement failed, according to its leaders, for two reasons, both of which are rapidly diminishing:

1) **Rural isolation and passivity.** The farm sector is acquiring modern communications and is investing its growing capital in rural industry, increasingly linked to towns and cities, while migration to the cities is explosive. The industrial sector has outgrown the agricultural, and is steadily drawing ahead.

2) **State control of the individual.** Private industry uses short-term labor contracts and work standards conducive to labor mobility, and wage rates affording independence from State subsidies on which security sanctions are based. As these conditions of work become steadily more general, State control of the individual is declining.

The Party remains in power, but its Marxist ideology is in disarray and has lost credibility in all sectors of society, while Party leaders themselves (and leaders of the military forces) are heavily involved in private enterprise and the world market. So, the destination seems far less in doubt than the timing.

China is not menacing its neighbors, as witness the settlement of frontier disputes with India and Siberia. Nor has China exercised its UN veto to hamper peacekeeping or the rule of law, while differences over armament issues are routinely negotiated.

The US needs, and apparently is receiving, Beijing's cooperation on Korean issues as well as its continued restraint in respect to Taiwan. Much foreign investment in China today, perhaps half, comes from South Korea, Taiwan and Hong Kong. This quiet but powerful process is strengthening mutuality between China and potential points of tension on its frontiers.

We gain little by threatening trade sanctions over internal matters which are evolving appropriately, if in a Chinese manner. Trade and investment are in fact the prime drivers of social and political changes that draw China into a community of interest in stability of the world and in time a more open domestic society.

Ahead in China lies a tremendous future weight in world affairs of every kind. The crucial task of this decade is assimilation of China into the world order as a major and responsible partner. The good news is that this is happening, in remarkably good order, because it is China's own objective as well as ours.

More About the Authors

The authors of this book, from the generation formed in its youth by World War II, are graduates of Yale (Green), Columbia and Chicago (Stokes), and West Point (Holdridge), then officers in the Navy (Green), Air Force (Stokes) and Army (Holdridge). They were married in wartime and have several children, born in the US and at posts abroad.

They entered the Foreign Service in their twenties, directly from the military, and served in East Asia with language competence in Japanese (Green) and Chinese (Stokes and Holdridge). They have been decorated by the State Department for exceptional service.

APPENDIX

SHANGHAI COMMUNIQUE, FEBRUARY 28, 1972

(*Department of State Bulletin,* Vol. LXVI, No. 1708 [March 20, 1972,] pp. 435-438.)

President Richard Nixon of the United States of America visited the People's Republic of China at the invitation of Premier Chou Enlai of the People's Republic of China from February 21 to February 28, 1972. Accompanying the President were Mrs. Nixon, U.S. Secretary of State William Rogers, Assistant to the President Dr. Henry Kissinger, and other American officials.

President Nixon met with Chairman Mao Tse-tung of the Communist Party of China on February 21. The two leaders had a serious and frank exchange of views on Sino-U.S. relations and world affairs.

During the visit, extensive, earnest and frank discussions were held between President Nixon and Premier Chou En-lai on the normalization of relations between the United States of America and the People's Republic of China, as well as on other matters of interest to both sides. In addition, Secretary of State William Rogers and Foreign Minister Chi P'eng-fei held talks in the same spirit.

President Nixon and his party visited Peking and viewed cultural, industrial and agricultural sites, and they also toured Hangchow and Shanghai where, continuing discussions with Chinese leaders, they viewed similar places of interest.

The leaders of the People's Republic of China and the United States of America found it beneficial to have this opportunity, after so many years without contact, to present candidly to one another their views on a variety of issues. They reviewed the international situation in which important changes and great upheavals are taking place and expounded their respective positions and attitudes.

The U.S. side stated: Peace in Asia and peace in the world requires efforts both to reduce immediate tensions and to eliminate the basic causes of conflict. The United States will work for a just and secure peace: just, because it fulfills the aspirations of peoples and nations for freedom and progress; secure, because it removes the danger of foreign aggression. The United States supports individual freedom and social progress for all the peoples of the world, free of outside pressure or intervention. The United States believes that the effort to reduce tensions is served by improving communication between countries that have different ideologies so as to lessen the risks of confrontation through accident, miscalculation or misunderstanding. Countries should treat each other with mutual respect and be willing to compete peacefully, letting performance be the ultimate judge. No country should claim infallibility and each country should be prepared to re-examine its own attitudes for the common good. The United States stressed that the peoples of Indochina should be allowed to determine their destiny without outside intervention; its constant primary objective has been a negotiated solution; the eight–point proposal put forward by the Republic of Vietnam and the United States on January 27, 1972 represents a basis for the attainment of that objective; in the absence of a negotiated settlement the United States envisages the ultimate withdrawal of all U.S. forces from the region consistent with the aim of self-determination for each country of Indochina. The United States will maintain its close ties with and support for the Republic of Korea; the United States will support efforts of the Republic of Korea to seek a relaxation of tension and increased communication in the Korean peninsula. The United States places the highest value an its friendly relations with Japan, it will continue to develop the existing close bonds. Consistent with the United Nations Security Council Resolution of December 21, 1971, the United States favors the continuation of the ceasefire between India and Pakistan and the withdrawal of all military forces to within their own territories and to their own sides of the ceasefire line in Jammu and Kashmire; the United States supports the right of the of the peoples of South Asia to shape their own future in peace, free of military threat, and without having the area become the subject of great power rivalry.

The Chinese side stated: Wherever there is oppression, there is resistance. Countries want independence, nations want liberation and the people want revolution — this has become the irresistible trend of history. All nations, big or small, should be equal; big nations should not bully the small and strong nations should not bully the weak. China will never be a superpower and it opposes hegemony and power politics of any kind. The Chinese side stated that it firmly supports the struggles of all the oppressed people and nations for freedom and liberation and that the people of all countries have the right to choose their social systems according to their own wishes and the right to safeguard the independence, sovereignty and territorial integrity of their own countries and oppose foreign aggression, interference, control and subversion. All foreign troops should be withdrawn to their own countries.

The Chinese side expressed its firm support to the peoples of Vietnam, Laos and Cambodia in their efforts for the attainment of their goal and its firm support to the seven-point proposal of the Provisional Revolutionary Government of the Republic of South Vietnam and the elaboration of February this year on the two key problems in the proposal, and to the Joint Declaration of the Summit Conference of the Indochinese Peoples. It firmly supports the eight-point program for the peaceful unification of Korea put forward by the Government of the Democratic People's Republic of Korea on April 12, 1971, and the stand for the abolition of the "U.N. Commission for the Unification and Rehabilitation of Korea." It firmly opposes the revival and outward expansion of Japanese militarism and firmly supports the Japanese people's desire to build an independent, democratic, peaceful and neutral Japan. It firmly maintains that India and Pakistan should, in accordance with the United Nations resolutions on the India-Pakistan question, immediately withdraw all their forces to their respective territories and to their own sides of the ceasefire line in Jammu and Kashmir and firmly supports the Pakistan Government and people in their struggle to preserve their independence and sovereignty and the people of Jammu and Kashmir in their struggle for the right of self-determination.

There are essential differences between China and the United States in their social systems and foreign policies. However, the two sides agreed that countries, regardless of their social systems, should conduct their relations on the principles of respect for the sovereignty and territorial integrity of all states, non-aggression against other states, non-interference in the internal affairs of other states, equality and mutual benefit, and peaceful coexistence. International disputes should be settled on this basis, without resorting to the use or threat of force. The United States and the People's Republic of China are prepared to apply these principles to their mutual relations.

With these principles of international relations in mind the two sides stated that:

-progress toward the normalization of relations between China and the United States is in the interests of all countries;

-both wish to reduce the danger of international military conflict;

-neither should seek hegemony in the Asia-Pacific region and each is opposed to efforts by any other country or group of countries to establish such hegemony; and

-neither is prepared to negotiate on behalf of any third party or to enter into agreements or understandings with the other directed at other states.

Both sides are of the view that it would be against the interests of the peoples of the world for any major country to collude with another against other countries, or for major countries to divide up the world into spheres of interest;

The two sides reviewed the long-standing serious disputes between China and the United States. The Chinese side reaffirmed its position: The Taiwan question is the crucial question obstructing the normalization of relations between China and the United States; the Government of the People's Republic of China is the sole legal government of China; Taiwan is a province of China which has long been returned to the motherland; the liberation of Taiwan is China's internal affair in which no other country has the right to interfere; and all U.S. forces and military installations must be withdrawn from Taiwan. The Chinese Government firmly opposes any activities which aim at the creation of "one China, "one Taiwan," "one China, two governments," "two Chinas," and "independent Taiwan" or advocate that "the status of Taiwan remains to be determined."

The U.S. side declared: The United States acknowledges that all Chinese on either side of the Taiwan Strait maintain there is but one China and that Taiwan is a part of China. The United States Government does not challenge that position. It reaffirms its interest in a peaceful settlement of the Taiwan question by the Chinese themselves. With this prospect in mind, it affirms the ultimate objective of the withdrawal of all U.S. forces and military installations from Taiwan. In the meantime, it will progressively reduce its forces and military installations on Taiwan as the tension in the area diminishes.

The two sides agreed that it is desirable to broaden the understanding between the two peoples. To this end, they discussed specific areas in such fields as science, technology, culture, sports and journalism, in which people-to-people contacts and exchanges would be mutually beneficial. Each side undertakes to facilitate the further development of such contacts and exchanges.

Both sides view bilateral trade as another area from which mutual benefit can be derived, and agreed that economic relations based on. equality and mutual benefit are in the interest of the people of the two countries. They agree to facilitate the progressive development of trade between their two countries.

The two sides agreed that they will stay in contact through various channels including the sending of a senior U.S. representative to Peking from time to time for concrete consultations to further the normalization of relations between the two countries and continue to exchange views on issues of common interest.

The two sides expressed the hope that the gains achieved during this visit would open up new prospects for the relations between the two countries. They believe. that the normalization of relations between the two countries is not only in the interest of the Chinese and American peoples but also contributes to the relaxation of tension in Asia and the world. President Nixon, Mrs. Nixon and the American party expressed their appreciation for the gracious hospitality shown them by the Government and people of the People's Republic of China.

INDEX

To order additional copies of this book
photocopy and return the form below.